Aurea Vidyā Collection*

——— 7 ———

*For a complete list of Titles, see page 95.

ātmabodha

This book was originally published in Italian
as, *Ātmadodha* in, Śrī Śaṅkarācārya, *Opere Minori*, Vol. II, Edizioni Āśram Vidyā, Rome.

First published in English in 2003
by Aurea Vidyā.
39 West 88th Street, New York, N.Y., U.S.A.
www.vidya-ashramvidyaorder.org

Set in font ©Vidyā 11/13 points by Aurea Vidyā

Printed and bound by Lightning Source Inc. at locations in the U.S.A. and in the U.K., as shown on the last page.

ISBN 1-931406-06-5
Library of Congress Control Number: 2003097659

On the cover: "Corno – Quod est Inferius est sicut quod est Superius, et quod est Superius est sicut quod est Inferius – 1307-2003" Detail.

Author: AM. Private Collection.

Śaṅkara

ātmabodha

Self-Knowledge

Translation from the Sanskrit, and Commentary, by

RAPHAEL

(Āśram Vidyā Order)

AUREA VIDYĀ

I bow to that yoga, taught by the very Scriptures, well known as Asparśa, free from relations, beneficial, generator of bliss for all beings, and free of oppositions and contradictions.

Gauḍapāda

TABLE OF CONTENTS

PREFACE

This edition of *ātmabodha*, which is here presented in English, has been translated directly from Sanskrit and edited and commented by Raphael.

His commentary on Śaṅkara's *śloka* is based on the following criteria:

a) To remain faithful to the *Advaita* and *Asparśa* Tradition to which the text belongs.

b) To make the text accessible to the Western reader by using a conceptual methodology that harmonizes with the Western mind structure and its receptiveness. To do this without impoverishing, vulgarizing, nor forcing *Advaita* into a "system".

c) To stimulate the reader's consciousness in an appropriate way, considering that Raphael is a living and practicing *advaitin-asparśin*.

In the Traditional view only the Doctrine itself has value, not the individual presenting it. It is for this reason that Raphael focuses on an effective transmission of the Teaching, shunning all desire to express personal views concerning the Doctrine. He is a faithful interpreter and concentrates his efforts on providing incisive and clear comprehension of the Doctrine.

Every authentic traditional conception should not be the object of simple erudition but of life experience.

«When we speak of realizative Philosophy» says Raphael «this means that it has to be experienced and not memorized. It must be a way of living and being. "Experiencing" consists in a process of absorption into consciousness in order to become one with Truth. We should not forget that Truth is disclosed in order to be meditated upon, assimilated and lived by: it has no other purpose... To consider Traditional Philosophy in any other way means distorting its raison d'être and degrading it to a mere intellectual pastime».

Śaṅkara and the *Advaita Vedānta*

The whole Hindu Tradition is essentially founded on the *Veda*, meaning Sacred Science and Traditional Knowledge par excellence. The diverse metaphysical and cosmological conceptions of India are not at all incompatible with each other. They are developments, *darśana* (perspectives), of the one doctrine which is constituted by the *Veda*, the principle and foundation of all the derived Branches.

Vedānta, etymologically "end of the *Veda*", is one of the six *darśana* of Hindu spirituality and is based on the teaching of the *Upaniṣad*, which are themselves an integral part of the *Veda*. The expression "end of the *Veda*" must be taken in its double meaning of "conclusion" and "aim", in that the *Upaniṣad* are the final part of the *Veda*, and their Teaching is the ultimate aim of the entire Traditional Knowledge.

Within *Vedānta* three different currents are identifiable: the *Advaita Vedānta* (non-dualism) codified by Śaṅkara, the

Viśiṣṭādvaita (qualified monism) codified by Rāmānuja and the *Dvaitavedānta* (dualism) codified by Madhva.

These three perspectives should not be viewed as opposing one another, but rather as corresponding to the position of consciousness attained by each codifier, enabling each to "see" respectively the dual, monistic or *non-dual* aspect in the *Śruti*.

The *Advaita Vedānta*[1] is a purely metaphysical doctrine which transcends religious dualism as well as ontological monism. Its fundamental theme is the search for the Absolute, *Brahman*. Thus, *Advaita Vedānta* constitutes *brahmavidyā*, knowledge of *Brahman*, and it is essentially characterized as *Advaitavāda*, "the Doctrine of Non-duality". In the *Advaitavāda*, *Brahman*, the supreme Principle, is referred to as "without-a-second", because it is beyond any determination.

Based on Raphael's writings, a synthesis of the *Advaita* follows, with special reference to several of its founding principles. These founding principles have often been interpreted following the letter rather than the spirit of Śaṅkara's which has given rise to misunderstandings and misconceptions.

The essence of the *Advaita* teaching is contained in this "simple" statement:

«*Brahman* is the only Reality, the world is non-real and "That thou art" (*Tat tvam asi*)»[2].

---

[1] For a further research on the *Advaita Vedānta*, cp., Gauḍapāda, *Māṇḍūkyakārikā*, translated from the Sanskrit, and commented, by Raphael. Aurea Vidyā, New York.

Also cp., Raphael, *Tat tvam asi* (That thou art). Aurea Vidyā, New York, and, Raphael, *The Pathway of Non-Duality*. Motilal Banarsidass, Delhi.

[2] *Chāndogya Upaniṣad*: VI, VII, 7. Edizioni Āśram Vidyā. Rome. [Italian Edition].

According to *Advaita Vedānta*, Reality must be constant, identical to itself, self-demonstrable, indivisible, infinite, and outside of space-time-causality. Furthermore, *Vedānta* develops its examination of the Real through all systems of coordinates and on all levels of Being, from the individual to the universal.

Stating that «*Brahman* is the sole Reality» could be taken as implying that all the rest is "illusion". This objection has often been raised and continues to be raised with regard to Śaṅkara's doctrine.

The question, though, should be put in a different way, i.e.: if *Brahman* alone is the sole Reality, then what is it that which we see and perceive?

In his commentary to Gauḍapāda's *Kārikā* to the *Māṇ ḍūkya Upaniṣad*, Śaṅkara affirms: «...this duality is nothing but *māyā*, also called the phenomenal world»[1].

The term *māyā* has many different meanings: "what makes the impossible possible", "taking something for something else", "veiling superimposition", etc. In western terms we would say that, for Śaṅkara *māyā* corresponds to what we would call "appearance", "(changing) phenomena", "conformed movement (that which shapes forms)".

Using Śaṅkara's example, we mistake the rope for a snake because of *māyā*. We superimpose one datum on another. This fundamental problem of "superimposition" (*adhyāropa*) and of "substitution" (*adhyāsa*) has been examined by Śaṅkara in his "Introduction" to his Commentary of the *Brahmasūtra* of Bādarāyaṇa.

---

[1] *Māṇḍūkya Upaniṣad* with Gauḍapāda's *Kārikā* and Śaṅkara's Commentary: I, 17. Edizioni Aśram Vidyā, Rome. [Italian edition].

It must be noted that *māyā* is not a *substantial* reality, which may disappear and be replaced by yet another substantial reality. In order to eliminate the snake seen in place of the rope, all that needs be done is to open the eye of vision (knowledge). Similarly, in order to make a mental representation disappear, it is only necessary to still the mind.

Furthermore *māyā* is not "illusion", which is the meaning ascribed to it in the West. Some people have even described Śaṅkara's doctrine, also at times in disparaging terms, as illusionism. An illusion in the strict sense of the term, produces nothing, is non-existent; an illusory event is comparable to the "horns of a hare", while Śaṅkara maintains that the *māyā*-universe is not like the "horns of a hare" or the "child of a barren woman"[1].

If an event or a datum is able to modify our pre-existing state of consciousness it cannot be called illusion. That snake which modifies our consciousness surely had a starting point or a real base in order to subsist. It cannot be born of nothing. Its base is in effect the rope (reality).

The are considerations above are important in order to comprehend *māyā* correctly and in the context of Traditional *Advaita*. In fact, its erroneous interpretation may lead the individual to a stance that could develop into nihilism, according to which everything, subject, object and the substratum of both is reduced to nothingness. Such a statement is refuted by *Vedānta*, which affirms that everything can be negated except the ultimate Witness which is negating. All can be doubted, except the ultimate Subject which is doubting. All

---

[1] Gauḍapāda, *Māṇḍūkyarika*, IV, 40; III, 28. Op. cit.

can be seen appearing and disappearing, except the knowing Witness of the seesaw of *saṁsāra*.

If we refer to the spirit rather than the letter of Śaṅkara's doctrine, we can see that *Advaita Vedānta* maintains that, all that belongs to the process of becoming, together with its implications, *has its value and degree of truth only as long as one is involved in the process*.

Thus our life, as we conceive of it within our empirical, distinctive sphere of existence, has its value as long as we are in it, but it becomes obvious that one who is on the outside no longer attributes any absoluteness to it.

Here again Śaṅkara has posed the problem correctly: the empirical world has its meaning and its raison d'être as long as we are identified with it.

Every human action, ethics, research, etc., has its meaning as long as we experience a life of relations or individuality. But, since this life is not absolute, as it is based only on a relative degree of truth, then sooner or later we will have to become aware of something deeper in the presence of which all that is relative loses importance, just as a dream loses importance when one awakens. In the waking state nobody would dare to mourn the dead seen in a dream or pay attention to speeches heard in a dream, nor would one count on a treasure discovered in a dream.

The metaphysics of Non-duality does not suggest to disregard or deny *māyā*, as such an attitude would also fall within *avidyā*. *Advaita* is saying that one ought not to create identification or identity with *māyā*, nor superimpose *māyā* on Reality, mistaking thus the rope for a snake.

From this metaphysical perspective, life cannot be in opposition with anything or anybody, because in this vision both the phenomenon and the noumenon are resolved into the One-without-a-second.

Some see in *Advaita Vedānta* a sort of "philosophical phenomenism", others equate it to "pantheism (immanentism)" while others identify it with a form of idealism, "subjective idealism" or "objective idealism".

It seems therefore necessary to write a few notes on these philosophical positions highlighting their differences with *Advaita Vedānta*.

"Philosophical phenomenalism" maintains that all is phenomenon, including Reality itself as well as the individual in its totality. Śaṅkara asserts instead that behind the phenomenon exists the Reality which is not phenomenon, and this Reality constitutes the Constant, without birth, time, space and causality. Behind the phenomenon-*māyā* is *Brahman*, both Absolute and Infinite. To state that Reality is relative appearance-phenomenon and change is not in accordance with reason, if only for the simple fact that if all is relative and mutable, the statement "all is relative" is also relative. Phenomenalism thus postulates a contradiction, that of *absolute relativism*.

"Pantheism" states that all is nature, that a transcendent Entity does not exist, that all is immanent in absolute terms and that Deity exhausts itself in the World. This is not in agreement with *Advaita*. According to *Advaita* a situation of non-reciprocity exists in the relationship of *Brahman* to the World. «*Brahman*, in truth, is other than the [sensible-intelligible] universe, [however] nothing else exists outside of *Brahman*. Wherever something other than *Brahman* appears to be manifest, it is fallacious, just like the apparition of a mirage in the desert». (*ātmabodha*, 63).

"Subjective idealism" negates external material reality altogether and takes everything back to one's own individual consciousness. Because it recognizes only the subjective idea of the single individual as real, this vision results in a dangerous solipsism.

"Objective idealism" posits the object as independent of the perceiving subject. It makes everything depend on the object, whether individual or universal.

The last two philosophical currents, subjective and objective idealism, cannot be confused with *Advaita Vedānta*. According to *Advaita*'s metaphysical Doctrine, although both the individual and the universal are each accorded a degree of reality, they resolve into the *Brahman*-Absolute.

The *ātmabodha* in Śaṅkara's Work

The works of Śaṅkara can be classified in three main groups:

– *Bhāṣya* or "Commentaries" on the fundamental texts that constitute *Vedānta*'s "Threefold Science" (*prasthānatraya*): the *Upaniṣad*, the *Brahmasūtra* and the *Bhagavadgītā*.

– *Stotra*, devotional chants and hymns of praise;

– *Prakaraṇa*, works or specific treatises in prose and in verse, explaining some passages of the Scriptures.

Ātmabodha (*ātma*-Knowledge) is a well-known *prakaraṇa* upon which many students of *Vedānta* have written commentaries. The explanation of the terms and expressions utilized in the Scriptures is useful for the student's comprehension of the subtle themes that are often hidden there.

The knowledge of this introductory text becomes, therefore, an essential prerequisite for those who want to comprehend *Advaita Vedānta*.

Śaṅkara addresses those who have purified themselves through the practice of austerity (*tapas*), attained peace in their hearts *(śāntānām)*, are liberated from all fear, are freed from the desires of the senses (*vītarāgiṇām*) and now aspire to just one thing: identity with the Being-without-a-second (*mumukṣutva*).

For *Advaita Vedānta* what imprisons us is *avidyā* or metaphysical ignorance. It is therefore only through "knowledge" of a metaphysical order that we can defeat ignorance concerning the nature of Being. This Knowledge implies a deep transformation, a realizative *sādhanā* whose phases are only moments of transformation-transfiguration of the entity following the unfolding of realizations, i.e. "recognitions". And this is so because the entity is already in itself absolute Consciousness.

The qualifications for the aspirant are: discernment (*viveka*) between Real and non-Real, detachment (*vairāgya*) from the non-Real, which is recognized as such, the six mental virtues, and *mumukṣutva*, which is the burning aspiration to Liberation[1].

If the "aspiration" or "love for Liberation" is missing, the final aim cannot be attained and in this regard Śaṅkara states:

> «Aspiration to Liberation is characterized by an intense yearning towards the dissolution of the ties of life through

[1] Cp., Śaṅkara, *Vivekacūḍāmaṇi*, *sūtra* 19 and following. Aurea Vidyā. New York.

the realization of the identity of the *ātman* with *Brahman*. Love for Realization is the basis for Liberation: if it is lacking the study and assimilation of the sacred Works will bear no fruit»[1].

Aurea Vidyā

[1] Śaṅkara, *Sarvavedāntasiddhāntasārasaṅgraha, sūtra* 226-227.

INTRODUCTION

Śaṅkara is considered one of the preeminent philosophical minds in the history of India. He realized the most perfect synthesis and harmonization of the entirety of Indian philosophical thought. His "method" for the research of Truth, which consisted primarily in liberating it from the veils that cover it, has given a contribution of great value to the metaphysical philosophical thought of the entire world.

He dedicated his brief but intense life (788-820) to the noble aim of "reviving " Vedic Tradition by re-establishing the authority of the *Śruti* (*Veda* and *Upaniṣad*) which in those times had been degraded.

To this end Śaṅkara compiled important Commentaries (*bhāṣya*) to the *Prasthānatraya* (*Upaniṣad*, *Brahmasūtra, Bhagavadgītā*), and also many other works. In the *Vivekacūḍāmaṇi*, the *Ātmabodha*, the *Aparokṣānubhūti* and the *Upadeśasāhasrī* he summarized both the teaching and the discipline by which to attain *Advaita* realization.

In his writings Śaṅkara placed the Vedic Scriptures on the highest philosophical plane by highlighting the non-dual (*advaita*) aspect already present in them. He established the Non-duality of the ultimate Reality with rigorous and profound investigation and with the most (abstract and) subtle analyses. He affirmed the greatness of this vision that he upheld not only in his "Commentaries" but also in philosophical disputes and in public debates, during which he raised objections to the theses of the representatives of other schools.

Śaṅkara came not to upset but to build, and the philosophy he taught should not be considered in opposition to the other schools of thought or *darśana*, in fact: «*Advaita* is a doctrine which does not come to vie with the other orthodox schools... but it illumines them from within and shows that a sole Truth polarizes the entire whole»[1].

By codifying *Advaita*, Śaṅkara has also furnished a firm ontological and metaphysical base for all the cults of the time by purifying their rituals and assuring their survival. By so doing he laid the foundations for a long-lasting and strong national unity.

Śaṅkara is considered from many perspectives a philosopher, a mystic, an exegete of the *Śruti*, a founder of monastic orders (*maṭha*), an *Avatār* (*Śiva*'s incarnation), a national hero. But above all he was the supreme Instructor (*Ācārya*) who was able to indicate the true and supreme end of human existence, based on Knowledge, and which constitutes the very aim of the *Upaniṣad*; the recognition of our own real nature and liberation *(mokṣa)* from *saṁsāra*-becoming.

«The central concern, the incandescent core of the entire and immense structure of Śaṅkara's thought, which has attracted and attracts multitudes of beings, is liberation... To be concerned first of all with this fundamental interest for liberation (*mokṣa*) is the safest way not to betray Śaṅkara... Respect for redeeming knowledge, which he welcomed as divine revelation (*Śruti*) occurred in remote, immemorial times, prompted Śaṅkara to transmit it as a living flame,

[1] P. Martin-Dubost, *Śaṅkara e il Vedānta*. Edizioni Āśram Vidyā, Roma, [Italian edition].

indeed not to mold it *ex novo,* thus impoverishing it... Śaṅkara pleased in defining himself, not as "supporter of *māyā*" as he is often characterized from many sides, but rather as "follower of the *Upaniṣad*" (*aupaniṣada*). In this very designation fidelity to the *Brahmanic* orthodoxy is fused with the consciousness of being the heir of the most precious heritage of man: i.e. knowledge of oneself, which resolves the world and its painful contradictions, because this is the meaning he assigns to the term "*Upaniṣad*"»[1].

In Śaṅkara we find an incredible combination of knowledge (*jñāna*), devotion (*bhakti*) and action (*karma*), three aspects which in him reach a splendid and complete maturation.

As a devout (*bhakta*) Śaṅkara was permeated by unlimited "compassion", faith and devotion. His genius was able to produce not only the most pure and abstract thoughts in order to affirm the philosophical doctrine of Non-duality, but also to create verses (*stotra*) full of ardor, like *Bhaja Govindam* and *Dakṣiṇāmūrtistotra*. Conscious that not all are in a position to undertake the metaphysical path which leads to *Brahman Nirguṇa*, Śaṅkara composed many devotional texts in praise of various Divinities. Among the hymns *Śivanandalaharī* stands out in poetic intensity, fervor and aesthetic beauty.

The combination of knowledge and devotion is already in itself a truly rare event, but in Śaṅkara it coexisted with another aspect as worthy of attention: untiring and dynamic action (*karma*) which placed him in an special position in the galaxy of immortal Sages, as the symbol of "triumphant acting". This prodigy of eternal wisdom was just sixteen

---

[1] M. Piantelli, *Śaṅkara e il Kevalādvaitavāda*. Edizioni Āśram Vidyā, Roma. [Italian edition].

when he started his work, traveling widely in the country. In the few years of his earthly life, he instituted ten monastic orders (*daśnāmin*) to prevent degenerations in the spiritual practice. He founded *maṭha*-monasteries at the four cardinal points of India. These *maṭha* were focal points of a most powerful Influx, which is experienced still today. Through these he assured the continuity of the Tradition.

«The Master (*Ācārya*) who has preached renunciation of the world, non-action, did not retire to a cave in the Himalayas, but traveled the country ceaselessly, wrote incessantly, instructed his disciples, and divulged the *Advaita* Doctrine».

This consideration of P. Martin-Dubost's is the best answer to those who maintain that Śaṅkara encouraged the individual toward total renunciation of the world.

Lastly Śaṅkara did not reject the ritual religion of the fathers, but lead the ritualistic *brāhmaṇa* to the comprehension of the relativity of their doctrines, as they had crystallized on some formal aspects of the one-Reality.

The *Śruti*, which is the foundation of religion itself, contains two aspects of the sole Reality, *para* and *apara*. These represent the *Brahman Nirguṇa*, without attributes, unqualified, and absolute, and the *Brahman Saguṇa*, the God-person with attributes. The sacerdotal order was anchored to the concept of the God-person, at times even disowning it, and also denying the supreme, and unqualified Reality without attributes, i.e. *Nirguṇa*.

In presenting *Advaita*, the principle of Non-duality, Śaṅkara proposed anew and brought to light the a-formal supreme Reality. Therefore, rather than conflicting with religion, he reaffirmed the complete Teaching of the *Śruti*.

R.

ātmabodha

tapobhiḥ kṣīṇapāpāṇāṁ śāntānāṁ vītarāgiṇāṁ |
mumukṣūṇām apekṣyo 'yam ātmabodho vidhīyate || 1 ||

1. *This ātmabodha [realization-Knowledge of the ātma]*[1] *has been composed for those who, yearning for Liberation, are fully purified from error (pāpa) through constant austerities (tapobhiḥ), and are pacified (śāntānāṁ) in their minds and free from desire.*

Śaṅkara highlights, right from the first *sūtra*, that his intention is to write for those who are qualified. Indeed *ātmabodha* is the quintessence of the *Advaita Vedānta* and therefore requires precise predispositions of psyche and consciousness on the part of the neophite.

Along the course of the *sādhanā*, many failures may occur because of a lack of those foundations or predisposing causes, which are indispensable in attaining specific realizative effects.

It is not sufficient to be good, in a sentimental way. It is not sufficient to have an emotional yearning for transcendence, or a keen and penetrating mind. What is needed is a *maturity* of consciousness and a deep-rooted "feel" for the Way of Return.

[1] Contents in square bracket along the text, are by the translator.

Therefore Śaṅkara addresses those who:

– Yearn for Liberation (*mumukṣutva*), which is the fruit of *maturity* of consciousness and not of escapism;

– Through ascesis or *tapas*, have purified their own hearts from those thoughts and actions which are not in accord with the universal *dharma*;

– Have attained mental calm (*śāntānām*) because all attraction-repulsion, which is the characteristic of an ego sentiment, has been mastered;

– Have prevailed over passion-desire (*vītarāgiṇāṁ*) for all objects, external and internal, material or ideal, being thus in a "dispassionate" state.

As one can see, just to realize this first *sūtra* alone, a whole lifetime is required. But we have to begin sometime, and those who are ready, no matter how difficult the present circumstances of their life may be, cannot but set themselves to work.

bodho 'nyasādhanebhyo hi sākṣānmokṣaikasādhanam ।
pākasya vahnivaj jñānaṁ vinā mokṣo na sidhyati ॥ 2 ॥

2. *As fire* [*is necessary*] *for cooking so, among the different types of discipline* (*vinā*), *only Knowledge* (*bodho*) *is the direct means for Liberation* (*sādhana mokṣa*): *without Knowledge there can be no Liberation.*

avirodhitayā karma nā 'vidyāṁ vinivartayet ।
vidyāvidyāṁ nihanty eva tejastimirasaṅghavat ॥ 3 ॥

3. *Since it is not in opposition to it, action cannot destroy ignorance; only Knowledge destroys ignorance, just as clear light dispels darkness.*

Why is it that only Knowledge can set us free? Because, according to *Advaita Vedānta*, *avidyā*, metaphysical ignorance, is what keeps us captive. Therefore only *vidyā*, metaphysical Knowledge, can defeat our ignorance as to the nature of Being. Darkness can be dispelled only by the splendor of light and error can be resolved only by truth.

Therefore, this cathartic, transforming knowledge, has the power to dissolve the erroneous perspective, in which the reflection of the incarnate *jīva* puts itself when it associates with the qualities (*guṇa*) of the bodies-vehicles.

There are *yoga* practices which may foster certain *samādhi*, or enable the individual (if we are allowed the expression) to converse with the Gods, may grant psychic powers and even offer realization of the principial One, but which cannot grant Liberation.

We should comprehend that Śaṅkara's *Advaitavāda*, like Gauḍapāda's *Asparśavāda*[1], aims exclusively at the realization of the metaphysical One, *Brahman Nirguṇa* (without attributes), the Constant, beyond time, space and cause. All human and superhuman states are but *māyā*, "conformed movement" (movement that creates forms).

Advaita is the path which transcends both *saṁsāra* and *nirvāṇa*, the manifest and the non-manifest (*avyakta*), the world of men and that of the Gods (*deva*). That is why integral Liberation is attained by means of Knowledge and

---

[1] For an in depth view of the *Advaita Vedānta*, also cp. Gauḍapāda, *Māṇḍūkyakārikā*. Op. cit.

not by psycho-physiological techniques or exercises, nor by acts, deeds or rites (*karman*) nor by a particular *mantra*.

These means may lead to the world of *Hiraṇyagarbha* (universal subtle state) or even to that of *Īśvara* (principial One) but, however lofty these worlds may be in comparison with the human state, they are nonetheless subject to the law of becoming, therefore to the law of *saṁsāra*. So, a clear distinction should be made between that which is integral Liberation and a universal expansion of consciousness.

The *advaitin*, like the *asparśin*, is not concerned with illness or physical health, psychic disharmony or harmony, ignorance or erudition, intellectual knowledge or material, psychic or divine power. He seeks only the Constant or *Brahman,* which is beyond all human and suprahuman bondage. This can be related to Plato's One-Good and to Plotinus' One.

paricchinna ivājñānāt tannāśe sati kevalaḥ ।
svayaṁ prakāśate hy ātmā meghāpāye 'ṁśumān iva ॥ 4 ॥

4. *It is precisely because of ignorance* (*ajñāna*), *that* [*the Self*] *appears to be in bondage. But once that* [*ignorance*] *is resolved, the ātmā shines forth and reveals itself absolute and free like the sun when it is no longer covered by clouds.*

When all mental projections, which are made up of all our family, cultural and social past, are eliminated, then the *ātman* will unveil in its essential nature.

ajñānakaluṣaṁ jīvaṁ jñānābhyāsād vinirmalam ।
kṛtvā jñānaṁ svayaṁ naśyej jalaṁ katakareṇuvat ॥ 5 ॥

5. *By means of constant practice in consciousness-knowledge, after perfectly purifying the individual soul [previously] clouded by non-knowledge, knowledge dissolves (svayaṁ), as does kataka powder after purifying the water.*

What needs to be done in order to realize the eternal and imperishable Self, the *ātman-Brahman*? It is necessary to dissolve the darkening clouds of ignorance that hide it.

The *ātman* is always such and certainly cannot change its nature. It only gets veiled by *māyā*'s power of projection. Knowledge represents the means to dissipate the clouds, and once they are dispelled, the *ātman* unveils of itself. Knowledge does not operate on the *ātman* but on the *avidyā-māyā*. When the boundless splendor of the *ātman* irradiates in its infinitude, both ignorance and Knowledge disappear, like the powder of the *kataka* nut after purifying the water.

Often we see a snake where there is only a rope, but Knowledge (*vidyā*) makes us comprehend that the snake is a *projection* and, from a certain perspective, it is nothing but the rope itself. In other words, the rope *appears* as snake.

Similarly, *Brahman* appears as *jīva*, *deva*, universe and so on, but *Brahman* is just *Brahman* beyond these superimpositions, like the rope is beyond the snake superimposition.

saṁsāraḥ svapnatulyo hi rāgadveṣādisaṅkulaḥ ।
svakāle satyavad bhāti prabodhe saty asad bhavet ॥ 6 ॥

6. *The world of becoming, characterized by attachment (rāga), repulsion (dveṣa), etc., is in fact similar to dream (svapna): it appears real as long as it lasts, it is revealed as unreal after awakening.*

tāvat satyaṁ jagad bhāti śuktikārajataṁ yathā ।
yāvan na jñāyate brahma sarvādhiṣṭhānam advayam ॥ 7 ॥

7. *As a shell of mother-of-pearl* [*appears*] *as silver, so the world appears real* (*satyaṁ jagad*) *as long as the non-dual* (*advayam*) *Brahman,* [*which is*] *beyond all* (*sarvādhiṣṭhānam*), *is not known.*

The world of becoming is nothing but "apparent movement", changing phenomena, ephemeral appearing and disappearing, similar to a dream that seems real when we are veiled by sleep, but not so when we wake up.

In dreams, every event, action, coming and going, every entry and exit, every image that one faces is not outside the dreamer's mind-consciousness. Similarly, at the macrocosmic level, every event-acting and every entity are not outside of *Īśvara*'s *Mahat*.

From this perspective, the world (*māyā*) is and is not. We cannot say that it is because everything, in effect, appears and disappears and we cannot say that it is not because something is perceived[1].

The analogies of the dream, the mirage, the magician's projection, the shell of mother-of-pearl taken for silver or the ray of light reflected on water etc. are quite enlightening and they give the idea of *saṁsāra*-becoming.

However, the universal phenomenon is not unreal or non-existent like the horns of a hare or the child of a barren woman (in Śaṅkara's examples). In fact, for the dreamer his dream is true and real. Only when he awakens does

[1] For further details on the subject cp., Raphael, *Tat tvam asi* (*That thou art*), ch. "Threefold Knowledge". Op. cit.

the dreamer realize that he experienced only an "apparent movement", devoid of absolute reality. In other words, a dream is a *degree* of truth that can be contradicted by another degree of truth and voided by still another one.

We could also speak of systems of coordinates that have their own validity-reality just within the limits of their apparition. So, for us inhabitants of the planet Earth, dawn and sunset are realities, but for a hypothetical inhabitant of the sun they possess no reality at all. For him, the problem does not even exist.

Upon awakening to the ultimate Reality, as permanent substratum, every system of coordinates (world of names and forms) disappears, as a dream recedes when waking comes[1]. This can be compared to Plato's "myth of the cave".

upādāne 'khilādhāre jaganti parameśvare |
sargasthitilayānyānti budbudānīva vāriṇi || 8 ||

8. *From the substantial foundation* (*adhāre*), *supreme Lord and first cause* (*upādāne*), *the worlds arise, are conserved* (*sthiti*) *and dissolve* (*laya*) *like foam bubbles in water* (*vāriṇi*).

«It is the supreme Lord, ... the Source of all; in it all things originate and dissolve»[1].

saccidātmany anusyūte nitye viṣṇau prakalpitāḥ |
vyaktayo vividhās sarvā hāṭake kaṭakādivat || 9 ||

---

[1] Gauḍapāda, *Māṇḍūkyarika*, VI. Op. cit.

9. *It is in the all-pervading and eternal Viṣṇu, Existence-Consciousness-Self, that all the different particular manifestations are represented [by the perceiver] like bracelets and other objects in gold.*

All of the unlimited micro and macrocosmic forms arise and are sustained through *materia prima*, represented by the *Mahat* or primordial *prakṛti* and therefore by *Viṣṇu*, and in it they dissolve. So, all ideas, concepts, images-forms arise from the mind, and in it they vanish.

yathākāśo hṛṣīkeśo nānopādhigato vibhuḥ ।
tadbhedād bhinnavad bhāti tannāśe kevalo bhavet ॥ 10 ॥

10. *As with ether, the all-pervading Lord, when associated with the various limiting and differentiated superimpositions* (*upādhi*) *appears as manifold, but unveils as absolute oneness when those are resolved.*

What establishes multiplicity are names and forms (*nāma-rūpa*). What differentiates the unity of the clay (*ākāśa*-ether or space is the example in the *sūtra*) are the various forms of jars. But, their formal and nominal multiplicity is apparent and not absolute-real. Looked at in the right light, the jars are just *modifications* of clay, just as the forms (bracelets, pins, rings, etc.) are nothing more than different expressions of gold.

By looking at things from an erroneous standpoint, some perceive formal multiplicity as split from the substantial unity. Some others, instead, see that multiplicity is an appearance of unity, or in other words, they see unity in multiplicity. The "identical in the diverse", according to Plato.

nānopādhivaśād eva jātivarṇāśramādayaḥ ।
ātmany āropitās toye rasavarṇādibhedavat ॥ 11 ॥

11. *It is precisely because of these manifold limitations that [ideas like] social order, descent, stages of life, etc., are superimposed on the Self, just as differences in taste, color, etc., [are perceived] in water.*

Social differences, color of skin or other differences, as well as the disciple's stages of life, social customs, etc., are just superimposed on the *ātman*. They are not absoluteness: they belong to the world of *māyā*, because they are the product of *nāma-rūpa*. The Awakened is beyond the various social orders (*varṇa*)[1] and beyond all *āśrama* (*brahmacārin, gṛhastha, vānaprastha, saṁnyāsin*)[2]. This implies that the Awakened has resolved into Unity-without-a-second, devoid of determinations, qualifications and distinctions.

pañcīkṛtamahābhūtasaṁbhavaṁ karmasañcitam ।
śarīraṁ sukhaduḥkhānāṁ bhogāyatanam ucyate ॥ 12 ॥

12. *Consisting of the five quintuplicated gross elements*[3] *and determined by its [own] past actions (karmasaṁcitam), the gross-physical body [waking state] is considered as the seat of the experience (bhoga) of pleasure and pain (sukhaduḥkha).*

---

[1] For *varṇa*, see *Glossary*.

[2] For *āśrama*, see *Glossary*.

[3] For the quintuplication process cp., Śaṅkara, *Pañcikaraṇa* and, Sureśvara, *Pañcikaraṇa-vārttika*.

pañcaprāṇamanobuddhir daśendriyasamanvitam |
apañcīkṛtabhūtotthaṁ sūkṣmāṅgaṁ bhogasādhanam || 13 ||

13. *Consisting of the five prāṇas (pañcaprāṇa), the empirical mind (manas), the buddhi (intellect) and the ten organs [of perception and action], and arising out of the five [subtle] non-quintuplicated elements, the subtle body is the instrument of experience [dream state].*

anādyavidyānirvācyā kāraṇopādhir ucyate |
upādhitritayād anyam ātmānam avadhārayet || 14 ||

14. *Ignorance, without beginning (anādi) and indefinable, is considered as the causal limitation-body. The ātman (Self) must be recognized as other than these three conditioning states.*

What we shall now consider are the so-called superimpositions, i.e. those limitations that veil the essence of being and make the One appear as manifold.

Three vehicles-bodies[1] "conceal" the *ātman*: these are, the gross body (*viśva*), the subtle body (*taijasa*) and the causal body (*prājña*). These bodies are cell aggregates at different degrees of condensation and represent the support, the instruments of relation or the windows that open on the various existential levels.

The gross or physical body (*annamaya*) is in relation with the material physical plane as we know it (*Virāṭ*) and through it we experience both physical and psychic dual-

[1] For the three bodies that hide the *ātman*, cp., Gauḍapāda, *Māṇḍūkyakārikā*. Op. cit.

ity. Those who are identified with this body interpret life in terms of matter, physicality, mass and the senses. Their consciousness is limited and confined exclusively to the plane of the vital "cortex".

The subtle body (*taijasa*) has three levels of reception: *prāṇa*, *manas*, and *buddhi*. Therefore the whole subtle sphere consists of the sheaths, or bodies of relation, *prāṇ amaya*, *manomaya*, and *vijñānamaya* or *buddhimaya*. They are made of more subtle energy, of hyperphysical substance, not visible to the human eye: they are sheaths that are to be found on other systems of coordinates.

The causal body (*prājña*) represents the germinal body, that of the first causes (*kāraṇopādhi*), from which the other bodies-sheaths are determined. It is called *ānandamaya*, body of bliss, because in it everything resolves into principial Unity, or *ākāśa*, and because in it the world of names and forms goes back to latency.

The being consists of these five bodies-sheaths, but the majority of people living at the physical level are so *polarized* with the *annamaya* (sheath made of food) that they recognize themselves only as physical entities. Hence the limitation, the prison and the materialistic vision of life.

The Self is other than these three limitations (*viśva*, *taijasa*, *prājña*). Using an analogy from the material level we know best, the *ātman* can be viewed as the nucleus in the atom system, while the sheaths are the various electronic elements. The nucleus, although different and equidistant from the electronic elements, gives life to the atom by its mere presence. By transferring this analogy, although improper, to the metaphysical plane, we can recognize the *ātman* as the self-shining polar sun that gives life to the various reception sheaths, simply by its presence. Of the two, the *ātman* and the vehicular complex, the first one is *sat-cit-ānanda* and is eternal, permanent, ever-present; the second one, instead, is a perishable, and limited phenomenon (*nāma* and *rūpa*). From the relationship between the *ātman* and the sheaths emerges that compound or entity called the individual, with a well defined qualitative configuration. Similarly, the atom-entity with its inherent qualities arises from the relation between the atomic nucleus and the electronic sheaths.

The "death" of a body-instrument-sheath does not impair the *ātman*, which, being absolute, lives of its own life. As an example, the pain that the individual usually experiences, with the loss of a physical body comes from his identification with that vehicle, from polarizing exclusively with it and seeing himself solely as body. The human being has still to comprehend himself in his totality. Though immortal as essence, due to a process of identification with relative and contingent phenomena (name and form), he believes himself to be mortal.

Liberation consists precisely in taking the reflection of the *jīva* back to its everlasting *ātman*-source.

We suggest again the diagram of the constitution of the being (see facing page) that we outlined in the commentary to the *Māṇḍūkyakārikā*[1].

pañcakośādiyogena tattanmaya imva sthitaḥ |
śuddhātmā nīlavastrādiyogena sphaṭiko yathā || 15 ||

---

[1] Gauḍapāda, *Māṇḍūkyakārikā*, II,19. Op. cit.

15. *In its identification with the five sheaths, etc., the pure Self appears as of their same nature, just like a crystal when placed over a blue cloth, etc.*

vapus tuṣādibhiḥ kośair yuktaṁ yuktyāvaghātataḥ ।
ātmānam antaraṁ śuddhaṁ vivicyāt taṇḍulaṁ yathā ॥ 16 ॥

16. *Just as a grain of rice, which at first is enveloped in its husk, etc., is totally separated from it, in the same way the pure inner Self must be discriminated through intelligent discernment from the sheaths with which it becomes identified.*

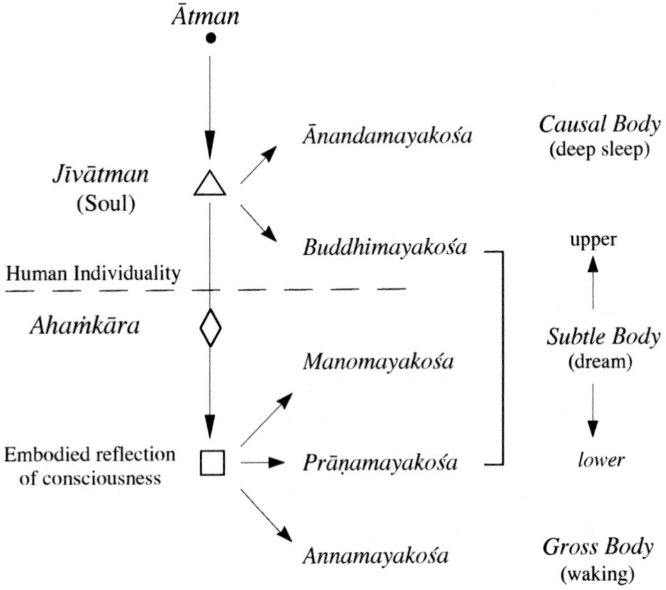

Like a crystal that reflects the colors of the environment, the Self or *ātman* seems to possess the qualities of the vehicles. Therefore, the reflection of the *ātman*-consciousness, identified with them, believes the *ātman* to be mortal, conflictual and dual. In other words, the individual assigns contingent qualifications to the Absolute; similarly, we usually attribute the color blue to the sky, and the limitations, above, below, inside, outside, etc., to space.

It is also from this standpoint that the limited individual being assigns to the Divinity qualifications that are instead inherent to his own specific state of consciousness.

In order to correct this error we need to realize, with the sword of discrimination and discernment, that the supreme Reality transcends the effect (*nāma-rūpa*) but also the cause (*ākāśa* or *prakṛti*).

sadā sarvagato 'py ātmā na sarvatrāvabhāsate ।
buddhāv evāvabhāseta svaccheṣu pratibimbavat ॥ 17 ॥

17. *Although it is ever all-pervading, the Self does not reveal itself everywhere. It manifests itself only in the pure intellect, just as a reflection* [*is perceived only*] *in a clear mirror.*

dehendriyamanobuddhiprakṛtibhyo vilakṣaṇam ।
tadvṛttisākṣiṇaṁ vidyād ātmānaṁ rājavat sadā ॥ 18 ॥

18. *The Self* (*ātman*) *must therefore be known – ever distinct from the body, senses, mind, intellect and prakṛti itself – as the Witness of their modifications, like a king.*

The *ātman* is reflected especially in the sheaths that are closer to it; that is in *ānandamaya* and *vijñānamaya*: windows open on the universal states of consciousness.

With the *manomaya* sheath the entity becomes individualized, separated from the universal context: it becomes "I am this" (*ahaṁkāra*). With such an attitude, truth is reversed: the contingent and apparent ego compound becomes reality and the *ātman* enters into oblivion.

vyāpṛteṣv indriyeṣv ātmā vyāpārīvāvivekinām ।
dṛśyate 'bhreṣu dhāvatsu dhāvann iva yathā śaśī ॥ 19 ॥

19. *Just as the moon appears to be running when the clouds move in the sky, similarly, to the non-discerning person, the Self appears to be active* (*ātmā vyāpāra*) *through the functions of the sense-organs* (*indriya*).

When the physical body or the mind are active we attribute this movement-activity to the Self. This constitutes the "error". The *ātman*-Self is the metaphysical foundation, the non-born thanks to which the vehicles can express themselves. But, while the *ātman*-Self can subsist also without the vehicles, these, instead, without That, cannot even be born and manifest.

It would be as if the sequences of the actions in a movie were attributed to the white screen, which stands as their *a priori* foundation and support, ever identical to itself.

ātmacaitanyam āśritya dehendriyamanodhiyaḥ ।
svakriyārtheṣu vartante sūryalokaṁ yathā janāḥ ॥ 20 ॥

20. *Just as men can work relying on sunlight, so when the body, the senses, the mind and the intellect (deha-indriya-manodhiyaḥ), in carrying out their respective functions, they depend on the consciousness inherent to the Self (ātmacaitanyam).*

dehendriyaguṇān karmāṇy amale saccidātmani |
adhyasyanty avivekena gagane nīlatādivat || 21 ||

21. *Due to lack of discernment, the functions and qualities of the body and senses are superimposed on the Self, which is absolute Existence and Knowledge, just as the color blue, etc., is attributed to the sky.*

ajñānān mānasopādheḥ kartṛtvādīni cātmani |
kalpyante 'mbugate candre calanādi yathāmbhasaḥ || 22 ||

22. *Due to the limitation constituted by the mind (mānasopādheḥ), functions such as actions and others are attributed to the Self through non-knowledge (ajñānām), just as the movement, etc., of the water [is attributed] to the moon reflected in it.*

As it is commonly conceived, movement is characteristic of the relative, the becoming and the phenomenon but, for the same reason already given, movement is attributed to what is beyond motion, beyond calm and beyond any form of duality. Motion and static conditions are always polar and they belong to the world of *māyā*. The individual in *saṁsāra* attributes ideals, actions, passions, aspirations, thoughts, good and evil to the *ātman*, which is devoid of cause and effect, time and space.

rāgecchāsukhaduḥkhādi buddhau satyaṁ pravartate ।
suṣuptau nāsti tannāśe tasmād buddhes tu nātmanaḥ ॥ 23 ॥

23. *In truth, attachment, desire, pleasure and pain, etc., arise when the intellect* [*buddhi*] *is present. In deep sleep, when it is not in existence, they too are not in existence. Hence, they belong to the buddhi and not to the Self.*

All of the qualities of the various *guṇa* belong to the vehicles which are constituted by the *prakṛti*-substance, substance from which all the forms of the micro and macrocosm are fashioned.

The *prakṛti* represents Plato's χώρα (chóra).

prakāśo 'rkasya toyasya śaityam agner yathoṣṇatā ।
svabhāvaḥ saccidānandanityanirmalatātmanaḥ ॥ 24 ॥

24. *Just as luminosity is the nature of the sun, coolness is of water and heat of fire, the nature of the ātman is absolute Existence-Consciousness-Bliss and eternal* (*nitya*) *purity* (*nirmala*).

The *ātman*, as a reflection of the supreme *Brahman*, is positive Reality not a vacuum, and it is not devoid of consciousness which reflects itself. Of the *ātman* one can say that it *is*. The bliss we are talking about is obviously not the sensorial one; it can be defined as "fullness" because it contains in itself all the containable.

ātmanaḥ saccidaṁśaś ca buddher vṛttir iti dvayam ı
saṁyojya cāvivekena jānāmīti pravartate ıı 25 ıı

25. *The notion "I know" is produced through the dyad – which stems from the absence of discernment – of Existence and Knowledge of the Self* (*ātmanaḥ*) *together with the modification* (*vṛttir*) *of the intellect.*

We were saying earlier that the *ātman* is the foundation of all that exists, therefore of the bodies-vehicles of manifestation and of their modifications (*vṛtti*). These modifications are superimposed (*uphādi*) on the *ātman* which is beyond any modification (*nivṛtti*), hence the very statement "I know" can be there because the light of the Self is there. Movement exists because it is determined by an immovable center. All polarities are interrelated and coexistent.

ātmano vikriyā nāsti buddher bodho na jātv iti ı
jīvaḥ sarvamalaṁ jñātvā jñātā draṣṭeti muhyati ıı 26 ıı

26. *In truth, no modification ever occurs on the part of the Self* (*ātmano*), *nor is knowledge in the least derived from the intellect. The reflection of the incarnate jīva who perceives all things from a false perspective, falls into error and considers itself as the one which knows and perceives* [*and acts*].

rajjusarpavad ātmānaṁ jīvo jñātvā bhayaṁ vahet ı
nāhaṁ jīvaḥ parātmeti jñātaś cen nirbhayo bhavet ıı 27 ıı

27. *By considering [erroneously] the reflection of the jīva as the Self* (*ātman*), *one is fear-stricken as in front of a snake perceived instead of the rope. If on the contrary, one thinks "I am not an individualized being, I am the supreme Self", one is freed from fear.*

The Self is also mistaken for an individual soul (*jīva*), for a contingent and transmigrating "product", whereby the *I am* consciousness is permeated with fear and conflict. The Self exists as the supreme reality, and all other things, which are considered as agents or attributes, are superimposed on the non-dual *ātman*.

From the interrelation of the reflection of pure Consciousness with the vehicle, arises the consciousness of the *I am*, i.e. of the *jīva* and of the individuality with a name and a form. The living soul (*jīva*) is a mere product that persists until there is identification with the vehicles and with the qualities the vehicles express. From the interrelation between the proton and the neutron arises the consciousness of the nucleus (this time assimilated to the *jīva*) and from the interrelation between the nucleus and the electrons the consciousness of the atom is born. However, both the nucleus and the atom (soul and individuality) are *phenomena* that vanish into pure elementary energy. This is, of course, just an analogy.

The *jīva* and the individuality are simple mirages that appear and disappear, that are and are not, that come and go, that express qualities and disappear into the non-qualified. The metaphysical error is to consider these two *ghosts* or shadows as absolute realities with a life of their own. The *jīva* is a ray of the *ātman* and operates at universal levels, while its reflection operates on the individual planes.

ātmāvabhāsayaty eko buddhyādīnīndriyāṇy api |
dīpo ghaṭādivat svātmā jaḍais tair nāvabhāsyate || 28 ||

28. *The Self alone illuminates the intellect, etc., as well as the senses (buddhyādīnīndriyāṇy), just as a lamp illuminates a jar, etc. One's own Self (svātmā) cannot be illuminated by those inert objects.*

svabodhe nānyabodhecchā bodharūpatayātmanaḥ |
na dīpasyānyadīpecchā yathā svātmaprakāśane || 29 ||

29. *For the Self, whose nature is Knowledge, there is no need for other means of knowledge in order to know itself, as a lamp does not need another lamp to illuminate itself.*

The *advaita* teaching that was given in the preceding several *sūtra*, is presented here in a synthesis:

1. Manifestation is a simple phenomenon; it is *māyā*, which produces the forms of becoming. From the perspective of the supreme Reality it can be compared to a dream, which is not nothingness, not the nil. It can be defined as contingent phenomenon, which appears on the horizon of Consciousness and disappears without leaving a trace. Therefore it can be defined as simple "appearance". This appearance stays real as long as the dreamer identifies with the dream; it reveals itself as non-real on awakening.

2. The *ātman* is the pure transcendent Witness, which, with a ray of its own consciousness, establishes itself in immanence.

3. The *jīvātman* is within its bodies-sheaths of manifestation. When it operates with the sheaths of *manas*, *kāma* and *deha* (gross physical body), it is in the individual state (*ahaṁkāra*); when it operates with the *buddhi* and *ānanda* sheaths, it is in the universal state.

4. What causes the *jīvātman* to be conditioned by the vehicles and by the qualities of the vehicles?

It is the *avidyā*, which is ignorance with regard to the real nature of being.

Identification with the sheaths' qualities (*guṇa*) obscures one's own nature. It corresponds to the myth of Narcissus. This kind of identification with what one is not represents *avidyā*. The reverse process consists in dis-identification and in *remembering* what one really is (Plato's remembrance), in putting our own wings back and flying towards that homeland that belongs to us (Plotinus).

Therefore the *jīva* may fall into the *error* of believing itself to be other than what it is, but not in an absolute manner, because it cannot change its immortal nature.

Parmenides makes *doxa* coincide with *error*, but in fact the entire Greek philosophy considers "opinion" as the source of error.

«From this way of search I keep you far», i.e. that *nothingness* may be, «but then also from the way along which the mortals who know nothing go wandering, two-headed; in fact indecisiveness in their hearts leads their senseless mind»[1].

Contradiction (two-headed) is typical of opinion, which is always dual, therefore not true.

For Plato himself δόξα is halfway in between Being and nothingness; in any case it is something non-positive. Only by attaining knowledge-science can one know opinion for what it is[2].

The preeminence given to *epistéme*, to which alone truth is exclusively connected, represents the thread for Pythagoras, Parmenides, Plato, Plotinus, etc., as well as for Gauḍapāda and Śaṅkara, as the *Māṇḍūkyakārikā* and this short treatise demonstrate.

If by an act of ignorance (*avidyā*) or non-knowledge we have "fallen" into generation, only by an act of knowledge (*gnosis*) we can be freed from error.

Therefore, through a process of negation (*neti-neti*) extended to all conditionings, individual and universal (identification with *sattva*), one attains the realization of the identity of the *jīva* with the *ātman* and of the *ātman* with the supreme *Brahman*, devoid of *guṇa* (*nir-guṇa*).

niṣidhya nikhilopādhīn neti netīti vākyataḥ |
vidyād aikyaṁ mahāvākyair jīvātmaparamātmanoḥ || 30 ||

30. *Through a [conscious] process of negation extended to all conditionings, by means of the axiom "not this, not this" (neti, neti) one has to attain, with the help of the great*

[1] Parmenides, *On the Order of Nature*, Edited by Raphael, Fr. 6, 4-5. Aurea Vidyā. New York.

[2] Cp. Plato, *Meno*, 96 d-e, 97, 98, 99a; and also , *Politeia*, V, 475a, 480.

aphorisms[1]*, the realization of the identity of the individual soul with the supreme Self.*

Through intuitive discernment we can recognize that all data-events are relative and dependent, and therefore we can say that the limiting sheaths are not (*neti, neti*) the Self, and that the individual soul itself (*jīvātman*) is only a reflection produced by the power of the Self.

At this point, if the preceding several *sūtra* have been assimilated, the *ācārya* Śaṅkara starts a series of *sūtra* to stimulate the reader's consciousness in a direct way to recognize itself as supreme reality beyond any phenomenal contingency.

«Because I am other than the body... Because I am other than the mind...», because I am without attributes and ever-existent, I am that supreme *Brahman* which is eternal, sole, and non-dual.

avidyākaṁ śarīrādi dṛśyaṁ budbudavat kṣaram |
etad vilakṣaṇaṁ vidyād ahaṁ brahmeti nirmalam || 31 ||

31. *Inasmuch as they are a product of ignorance, all that is perceived* (*dṛśyaṁ*)*, such as the physical body and other material objects, is as transient as a bubble of soap. One has, therefore, to realize consciously "I am Brahman"* (*ahaṁ brahmeti*)*, pure and different from all this.*

dahānyatvān na me janmajarākārśyalayādayaḥ |
śabdādiviṣayaiḥ saṅgo nirindriyatayā na ca || 32 ||

---

[1] For the *mahāvākya* or "great aphorisms", see the *Glossary*.

32. *Because I am other than the body, there are no such things for me as birth, old age, decay, death, etc., nor is there contact with the sense objects like sound and the others, for I have no sense organs* (*nirindriyatayā*).

amanatvān na me duḥkharāgadveṣabhayādayaḥ ǀ
aprāṇo hy amanāḥ śubhra ity ādiśrutiśāsanāt ǁ 33 ǁ

33. *As I am other than the mind, there are no such things in me as suffering, attachment, aversion, fear, etc. It [the Self] has no vital breath, nor mind; hence, it is pure, etc., as declared by the Scriptures* (*ādiśrutiśāsanāt*).

Attributing absoluteness to what is relative must be avoided. The Being is not the physical body, nor the conflicting mental one, nor anything else. It is pure and infinite Being, free from all imprisoning attributes. It is necessary to comprehend what is effect, what is cause and what is beyond the cause-effect polarity.

Fear, anxiety, sorrow, hope, desire, sensorial happiness, etc., are attributes of the ego-vehicles' compound, and not of the non-dual and eternally equanimous Self.

nirguṇo niṣkriyo nityo nirvikalpo nirañjanaḥ ǀ
nirvikāro nirākāro nityamukto 'smi nirmalaḥ ǁ 34 ǁ

34. *I am free from all attributes, devoid of movement, eternal, non-differentiated, untainted, changeless and formless, ever free and pure.*

aham ākāśavat sarvaṁ bahirantargato 'cyutaḥ |
sadā sarvasamaḥ śuddho nissaṅgo nirmalo 'calaḥ || 35 ||

35. *Everlasting, I pervade the inner and outer all, like the ether-space; I am forever identical in everything and at all times, perfect, absolute, immaculate and changeless.*

nityaśuddhavimuktaikam akhaṇḍānandam advayam |
satyaṁ jñānam anantaṁ yat paraṁ brahmāham eva tat || 36 ||

36. *Verily I am that supreme Brahman which is eternal, pure, free, sole, undivided bliss, non-dual, infinite Existence and Knowledge.*

«...that Being is non-born and incorruptible, in fact it is, in its entirety, whole, immobile and without end. Nor was it once, nor will it be, since it is now altogether everything, one and continuous. In fact, what birth for it will you be looking for? How and in what way would it have grown?»[1].

«This is *Brahman*'s eternal greatness: it does not grow, nor does it diminish»[2].

«...he will see all of a sudden a Beauty wonderful in its nature ...one which is above all eternal, which does not become nor does it perish and which does not grow or diminish»[3].

Therefore we can say with Parmenides:

---

[1] Parmenides, *On the Order of Nature*, Edited by Raphael, Fr. 8, 3-7. Op. cit.

[2] *Bṛhadāraṇyaka Upaniṣad*: IV, 23. Edizioni Āśram Vidyā. Rome. [Italian edition].

[3] Plato, *Symposium*: 210 E - 211 A. In, G. Reale. *Platone tutte le opere*. Bompiani. Milan. [Italian edition].

« For it [Being], all of those things the mortals established, convinced that they were true, are just names»[1].

evaṁ nirantarābhyastā brahmaivāsmīti vāsanā I
haraty avidyāvikṣepān rogān iva rasāyanam II 37 II

37. *Thus the meditation on "I am Brahman itself", practiced without interruption, destroys the projection movements of the mind caused by ignorance, just as medicine dispels illnesses.*

The *ātman* is one, indivisible bliss, eternal, at all times identical to itself, while its *reflections* are interacting phenomena.

Within conceptual bounds, it is possible to show this expressive sequence of the *ātman*:

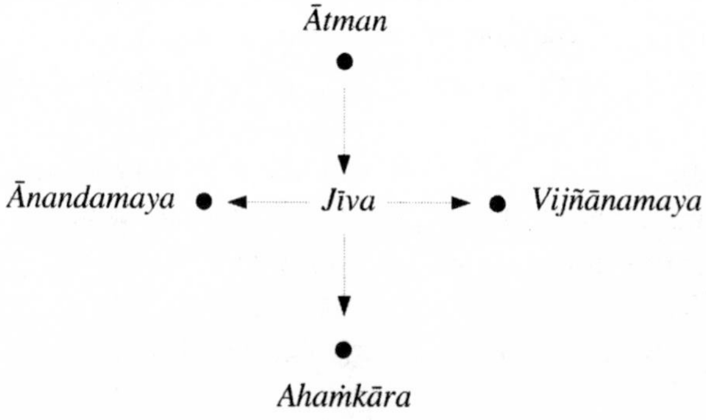

[1] Parmenides, *On the Order of Nature*, Edited by Raphael, Fr. 8, 38-39. Op. cit.

Ānandamaya and *vijñānamaya* are instruments of relation and of contact: their interrelation produces the "sense of ego" (*ahaṁkāra*).

So, just to use an analogy, the interrelation between hydrogen and oxygen generates water as the third factor.

The relation of the *jīvātman* with the vehicles happens through a process of polarization, while the return to the source happens through a process of de-polarization.

The *jīvātman*, or the *ahaṁkāra*, due to its intrinsic nature, can express itself along three directions:

a) Towards the object it has projected, identifying with it to the point of losing its identity. This is the condition of the majority of human beings. In fact they are deeply identified with the objective world, including the gross physical body (*annamaya*).

b) Towards the *agendi* subject (acting subject). This means to be detached from one's "dreams", "ideals" and from the world of objects in general. It is the optimal state on the plane of *māyā*. In other words, the subject is conscious of being cause or noumenon, and remains free from the vicissitudes of the effects.

c) Finally, it may re-orient itself towards its own source, which is the *ātman*, and resolve into the all-pervading Silence.

So, to further clarify the event of polarization we will say that the mind may: think (logic movement) and identify with its own thinking, think and remain free from its thought projections and, finally, it may not think at all and remain in its transcendent state[1].

---

[1] Cp., Gauḍapāda, *Māṇḍūkyakārikā*, Op. cit. pag. 30 and fwg. See also, chp. "The origin of subconsciousness" in, Raphael, *Tattvamasi* (That Thou Art). Op.cit.

viviktadeśa āsīno virāgo vijitendriyaḥ |
bhāvayed ekam ātmānaṁ tam anantam ananyadhīḥ || 38 ||

38. *Seated in a solitary place (vivikta), free from attachment (virāgo) and with the senses under control, [the disciple] must meditate on the ātman. One (ekam) and Infinite, without [making room for] any other thought (ananya).*

ātmany evākhilaṁ dṛśyaṁ pravilāpya dhiyā sudhīḥ |
bhāvayed ekam ātmānaṁ nirmalākāśavat sadā || 39 ||

39. *The Sage (sudhīḥ), with meditation (dhiyā), having dissolved (pravila) the entire perceivable (dṛśyaṁ) in the ātman, [must resume] the real state of the sole ātman, eternally pure (sāda nirmala) like the ākāśa.*

rūpavarṇādikaṁ sarvaṁ vihāya paramārthavit |
paripūrṇacidānandasvarūpeṇāvatiṣṭhate || 40 ||

40. *Having abandoned everything, such as form, social class, etc., the Knower of the supreme Reality is [definitively] absorbed in its own essence (svarūpa), [which is] infinite fullness (paripūrṇa) of Consciousness and Bliss.*

jñātṛjñānajñeyabhedaḥ pare nātmani vidyate |
cidānandaikarūpatvād dīpyate svayam eva hi || 41 ||

41. *In the supreme ātman a distinction (bheda) of knower, knowledge and object of knowledge cannot be found. Its nature (rūpa) is Consciousness-Bliss, [It] shines (dīpyate) by and of itself (svayam).*

evam ātmāraṇau dhyānamathane satataṁ kṛte |
uditāvagatir jvālā sarvājñānendhanaṁ dahet || 42 ||

42. *As fuel is entirely exhausted by the fire kindled by the churning of a rod, similarly ignorance is completely destroyed by constant meditation on the ātman* (*ātmā dhyāna*).

Seated in a propitious place, his consciousness free from material and psychical attachments, the ascetic should meditate exclusively on the Self, and avoid being conditioned by the movement of thoughts.

Through discernment (*viveka*) one must recognize the projective phenomena; then, through an act of dis-identification (*vairāgya*), it is necessary to depolarize the mind itself. So, all objects, phenomena, conventions, etc., lose importance and come to an end, just as the resolving fire exhausts all of its fuel.

In the supreme *ātman*-Self all distinctions, including that of knower, knowledge and object of knowledge, vanish.

aruṇeneva bodhena pūrvaṁ santamase hṛte |
tata āvirbhaved ātmā svayam evāṁśumān iva || 43 ||

43. [*When*] *the previous darkness* (*pūrvaṁ santamase*) *is dissolved* (*hṛte*) *by the solar illumination* (*aruṇa bodhi*), *the ātmā, like the sun, spontaneously* (*svayam*) *unveils* (*āvirbhaved*).

ātmā tu satataṁ prāpto 'py aprāptavad avidyayā |
tannāśe prāptavad bhāti svakaṇṭhābharaṇaṁ yathā || 44 ||

44. *The ātmā, though in truth ever-present, seems nevertheless absent because of ignorance; when ignorance is resolved, It unveils in all its presence just like an ornament on one's neck.*

When, through Knowledge, the various interrelations are burnt or depolarized, the *ātman* unveils by itself as does the sun when the clouds are gone, or when we discover that the ornament hanging from our neck was never missing.

Knowledge is necessary to comprehend the process of polarization and depolarization, so as to remove that veil (*māyā*) which obscures the reality of the Self. The Self was never missing, nor was it ever maimed by the dualism of *saṁsāra* or egoical play. In the same way the sun, although giver of life and motion, does not get involved in the vicissitudes of earthly activities.

sthāṇau puruṣavad bhrāntyā kṛtā brahmaṇi jīvatā ꠰
jīvasya tāttvike rūpe tasmin dṛṣṭe nivartate ꠰꠰ 45 ꠰꠰

45. *Just as a tree may be mistaken for a man (puruṣa), so, due to the same kind of error, Brahman is conceived as individual soul. But this [illusion] disappears once the jīva's true nature [as ātman] is recognized.*

tattvasvarūpānubhavād utpannaṁ jñānam añjasā ꠰
ahaṁ mameti cājñānaṁ bādhate digbhramādivat ꠰꠰ 46 ꠰꠰

46. *Knowledge derived from direct experience (ānubhava) of the nature (svarūpa) of Reality (tattva) immediately destroys ignorance which is characterized by the notions of*

"I" (ahaṁ) and "mine" (mameti), just as [it happens for] an erroneous cognition of orientation.

samyag vijñānavān yogī svātmany evākhilaṁ jagat |
ekaṁ ca sarvam ātmānam īkṣate jñānacakṣuṣā || 47 ||

47. *The Yogi, who has realized perfect Knowledge sees (īkṣate) with the eye of Knowledge (jñānacakṣus) the entire (sarvam) universe contained within himself and considers all things as the sole (ekaṁ) ātman.*

ātmaivedaṁ jagat sarvam ātmano 'nyan na vidyate |
mṛdo yadvad ghaṭādīni svātmānaṁ sarvam īkṣate || 48 ||

48. *This whole universe (jagat sarvam) is truly the ātman, nothing exists outside of the ātman. Just as any kind of pottery is nothing else but clay, in the same manner [the Knower] considers everything as himself (svātmānaṁ).*

The *Upaniṣad* says that we are drops of the same ocean, therefore we are ocean. The entire ocean-universe is contained in the drop and the drop in the ocean-universe. Behind the world of names and forms there is a sole Essence which permeates the totality of life. Behind the multiplicity of the forms (which are not) is Unity (which is). To see with the eye of wisdom (*jñāna*) means to see Unity in multiplicity.

jīvanmuktas tu tad vidvān pūrvopādhiguṇāṁs tyajet |
saccidānanadarūpatvād bhaved bhramara kīṭavat || 49 ||

49. *The Knower, who has abandoned all previous limiting conditions (upādhi) and their attributes (guṇa), thus unveiling its own nature of absolute Existence-Consciousness-Fullness, becomes a Liberated one in this life (jīvanmukta), like a chrysalis that turns into a butterfly.*

Earlier the Master Śaṅkara proposed the *Vedānta* Doctrine, the Vision one must refer to. Now, in the following several *sūtra*, he indicates the fruits that are obtained, once that Doctrine has been assimilated and integrated.

This *sūtra* shows the ultimate aim of Realization. The Liberated (*jīvanmukta*) is someone who has integrated and transcended all prior limiting conditionings: i.e. *avidyā* in its total expression.

tīrtvā mohārṇavaṁ hatvā rāgadveṣādirākṣasān ।
yogī śāntisamāyukta ātmārāmo virājate ॥ 50 ॥

50. *Having crossed the ocean of illusion (moha) and killed the demons (rākṣasa) of pleasure (rāga) and of repulsion-suffering, etc., the Yogi, in perfect oneness with Peace, shines with the Fullness of the ātman.*

bhāyānityasukhāśaktiṁ hitvātmasukhanirvṛtaḥ ।
ghaṭasthadīpavat svasthaḥ svāntareva prakāśate ॥ 51 ॥

51. *Renouncing with indifference any attachment to all fleeting external pleasures, fully satisfied with the bliss that proceeds from the Self, He shines inwardly as a lamp placed inside a jar.*

When the Being's consciousness shines in all its clearness, all projected ghosts disappear. Thus liberation from identification with what one is not occurs, even during life, i.e. even when we still wear our various bodies-vehicles, including the physical one. The vehicles do not *nullify* the *ātman*, but they can veil it when its reflection, *jīva* or *ahaṁkāra*, identifies with the various sheaths-bodies.

upādhistho 'pi taddharmair alipto vyomavan muniḥ |
sarvavin mūḍhavat tiṣṭhed asakto vāyuvac caret || 52 ||

52. *Although he lives immersed in the limiting conditionings, the Muni, like ether, is untouched by their attributes. One who truly knows all things lives* [*apparently*] *like a person devoid of intellect and, like the wind, moves around perfectly detached.*

upādhivilayād viṣṇau nirviśeṣaṁ viśen muniḥ |
jale jalaṁ viyad vyomni tejas tejasi vā yathā || 53 ||

53. *With the dissolution* (*vilaya*) *of the conditioning sheaths* (*upādhi*), *the Muni merges into the all-pervading Reality free from all differentiations* (*nirviśeṣa*), *like water in water, space in space or light in light* (*tejasi*).

So, although the ascetic finds himself within the limitations of the sheaths (*upādhi*), consciousness has nevertheless regained its absoluteness and recognized its identity with the uncontaminated *Brahman*, just as a ray of light recognizes itself as light and a drop of water as clear water.

yallābhān nāparo lābho yatsukhān nāparaṁ sukham ।
yajjñānān nāparaṁ jñānaṁ tad brahmety avadhārayet ॥ 54 ॥

54. *Realize Brahman as that attainment (yat) beyond which nothing else remains to be attained, beyond whose Bliss there is no other happiness (sukham), beyond whose knowledge there is no higher knowledge.*

In the several *sūtra* that follow, Śaṅkara exhorts us in a direct way to realize *Brahman* as That, which once "seen" nothing else is there to be seen; once known, nothing else is there to be known.

yad dṛṣṭvā nāparaṁ dṛśyaṁ yad bhūtvā na punar bhāvaḥ ।
yaj jñātvā nāparaṁ jñeyaṁ tad brahmety avadhārayet ॥ 55 ॥

55. *Realize Brahman as That which once seen nothing else remains to be seen, once realized, no further realization is there, once known, nothing else is there to be known.*

tiryag ūrdhvam adhaḥ pūrṇaṁ saccidānandam advayam ।
anantaṁ nityam ekaṁ yat tad brahmety avadhārayet ॥ 56 ॥

56. *Realize Brahman, which both in the high as in the intermediate space is Fullness (pūrṇa), as That which is absolute Existence-Consciousness-Bliss, pure Non-duality, Infinite, Eternal and One (ekaṁ).*

atadvyāvṛttirūpeṇa vedāntair lakṣyate 'dvayam ।
akhaṇḍānandam ekaṁ yat tad brahmety avadhārayet ॥ 57 ॥

57. *Realize that Brahman, which is indicated by Vedānta as the immutable Essence that unveils through the negation [of the superimpositions], as non-dual Unity of indivisible bliss.*

The individual has only one *dharma*: that of recomposing itself, rediscovering itself, finding itself. All its wandering, its *doings* are compensations; because *one is not*, one believes that by doing one is. And although one's incentive is right, the direction is wrong. Being can seek its true completeness only in Being.

One who lost a treasure, the sole source of life, will not have true peace unless and until it is found again. Only then will every search, movement, anxiety and ideal come to an end. Those who have realized themselves as *ātman* have nothing else to realize, those who have recognized themselves as *ātman* have nothing more to know. Who is in peace does not move, does not act and does not desire.

akhaṇḍānandarūpasya tasyānandalavāśritāḥ I
brahmādyās tāratamyena bhavanty ānandino 'khilāḥ II 58 II

58. *As they are dependent on a particle of bliss of That, whose nature (rūpa) is absolute and indivisible (akhaṇ ḍa) Bliss, all beings, from Brahmā on [to humankind and further], enjoy bliss to a greater or lesser measure [according to their degree of proximity to the supreme Reality].*

tadyuktam akhilaṁ vastu vyavahāras tadanvitaḥ I
tasmāt sarvagataṁ brahma kṣīre sarpir ivākhile II 59 II

59. *Every entity is intimately connected (yuktam) to That (tad), every manifestation is connected to That. Therefore Brahman pervades (sarvagataṁ) the whole totality as butter does milk.*

Every entity, from *Brahmā*, as causal Principle, to the individual being, unveils bliss in proportion to its more or less perfect identity with *Brahman*. All beings who experience the indefinite life modalities perceive *ānanda* (Bliss-Fullness) in proportion to their proximity to the supreme Reality, that Reality which is the substratum of every possible *māyā*-movement.

anaṇv asthūlam ahrasvam adīrgham ajam avyayam I
arūpaguṇavarnākhyaṁ tad brahmety avadhārayet II 60 II

60. *Realize Brahman, which is neither subtle nor gross, neither limited nor extended; non-born and indestructible, a-formal and without attributes (arūpaguṇa), devoid of qualifications and of designations.*

yadbhāsā bhāsyate 'rkādi bhāsyair yat tu na bhāsyate I
yena sarvam idaṁ bhāti tad brahmety avadhārayet II 61 II

61. *Realize that Brahman whose splendor (bhāti) sheds light on the sun and the other stars, but is not illuminated by their light, [that Brahman] thanks to whom alone all this [universe] is manifested.*

svayamantarbahirvyāpya bhāsayann akhilaṁ jagat I
brahma prakāśate vahnipratatptāyasapiṇḍavat II 62 II

62. *By comprehending in Itself all things external and internal, Brahman confers splendor, and in so doing makes itself manifest to the whole universe of phenomena, just like fire which, with its heat, makes a ball of iron red-hot.*

The *Brahman-ātman* cannot be conceived by mental categories because these are always characterized by subject-object; while the *ātman* is beyond every possible polarity and duality.

The *ātman* is not the eye, but that which enables the eye to see; the *ātman* is not the mind but that which enables the mind to exist and think; the *ātman* is not happiness nor bliss itself, but that which enables bliss-happiness to manifest and be; the *ātman* is not the sun, but that which enables the sun to rise and set.

jagadvilakṣaṇaṁ brahma brahmaṇo 'nyan na kiñcana |
brahmānyad bhāti cen mithyā yathā marumarīcikā || 63 ||

63. *Brahman, in truth, is other than the* [*sensible-intelligible*] *universe* (*jagadvilakṣaṇaṁ*), [*however*] *nothing else exists outside of Brahman. Wherever something other than Brahman appears to be manifest, it is fallacious, just like the apparition of a mirage in the desert.*

dṛśyate śrūyate yad yad brahmaṇo 'nyan na tad bhavet |
tattvajñānāc ca tad brahma saccidānandam advayam || 64 ||

64. *All that can be seen* (*dṛśyate*), *or heard* (*śrūyate*) *is nothing else but Brahman. But it is* [*only*] *through Knowledge of the supreme Reality that* [*one comprehends*

and realizes That], *that is, the non-dual Brahman, Existence-Consciousness-Bliss.*

Although *Brahman* is not the eye, the mind or the entire universe of names and forms, thus any pantheistic conception is excluded, nonetheless this entire mirage-phenomenon cannot appear without *That*.

sarvagaṁ saccidātmānaṁ jñānacakṣur nirīkṣate ।
ajñānacakṣur nekṣeta bhāsvantaṁ bhānum andhavat ॥ 65 ॥

65. *It is* [*only*] *through the eye of knowledge* (*jñāna-cakṣus*) *that the ātman, all-pervading Existence and Consciousness, can be contemplated. But if the inner sight is clouded by ignorance, It will never be known, as the shining* (*bhāsvantaṁ*) *sun* (*bhānum*) *cannot be seen by a blind man.*

śravaṇādibhir uddīpta jñānāgniparitāpitaḥ ।
jīvas sarvamalān muktaḥ svarṇavad dyotate svayam ॥ 66 ॥

66. *The individual soul, consumed by the fire of Knowledge* (*jñānāgni*) *kindled by audition* (*śravaṇa*) [*reflection and meditation*][1], *freed* (*muktaḥ*) *from all impurities* (*sarvamalān*), *shines of itself* (*svayam*) *like bright gold.*

hṛdākāśodito hy ātmā bodhabhānus tamo 'pahṛt ।
sarvavyāpī sarvadhārī bhāti bhāsayate 'khilam ॥ 67 ॥

---

[1] In order to gain Self-knowledge, the Teaching indicates a threefold practice (*śravaṇa*, *manana* and *nididhyāsana*) based on three successive phases: exposing the *sādhaka* (disciple) to the Scriptural Teaching imparted by a Master, reflection on the Master's delivery, meditation and assimilation thereon.

67. *In truth the ātmā, sun of Knowledge fixed in the space of the heart (hṛdākāśodito), is That which dispels darkness. Being the all-pervading substratum of all, It infinitely shines and makes everything shine.*

Only knowledge (*jñāna*) is liberating, because what veils and obscures consciousness is metaphysical ignorance (*avidyā* or *ajñāna*). There is no other means of liberation but that which knows how to break the chains of *saṁsāra*'s bondage. None else but the blazing sun can dispel the constraining darkness.

digdeśakālādyanapekṣya sarvagaṁ śītādihṛn nityasukhaṁ nirañjanam ।
yas svātmatīrthaṁ bhajate viniṣkriaḥ sa sarvavit sarvagato 'mṛto bhavet ॥ 68 ॥

68. *The being that renounces all activities and, free from all limitations of space, place, time, etc., pays devout homage to the sanctuary of his own all-pervading, untainted [ātmā] which is free from cold [and heat and from all other dualities] and is everlasting Bliss, this Being becomes omniscient, all-pervading, and immortal.*

The being that transcends time-space-cause (apparent movement) finds the hidden treasure again and enters into (this is only a figure of speech) the blissful sanctuary of the non-dual *ātman*.

ity ātmabodhaḥ samāptaḥ ॥
Here ends the work called
ātma-Knowledge

RAPHAEL

Unity of Tradition

Having attained a synthesis of Knowledge (with which eclecticism or syncretism are not to be associated), Raphael aims at "presenting" the Universal Tradition in its many Eastern and Western expressions. He has spent a substantial number of years writing and publishing books on spiritual experience and his works include commentaries on the *Qabbālāh*, Hermeticism and Alchemy. He has also commented on and compared the Orphic Tradition with the works of Plato, Parmenides and Plotinus. Furthermore, Raphael is the author of several books on the pathway of non-duality (*Advaita*), which he has translated from the original Sanskrit, offering commentaries on a number of key Vedantic texts.

With reference to Platonism, Raphael has highlighted the fact that, if we were to draw a parallel between Śaṅkara's *Advaita Vedānta* and a Traditional Western Philosophical Vision, we could refer to the Vision presented by Plato. Drawing such a parallel does not imply a search for reciprocal influences, but rather it points to something of paramount importance: a sole Truth, inherent in the doctrines and teachings of several great thinkers, who although far apart in time and space, have reached similar and in some cases even identical conclusions.

One notices how Raphael's writes from a metaphysical perspective in order to manifest and underscore the Unity of Tradition, under the metaphysical perspective. This does not mean that he is in opposition to a dualistic perspective, or to the various religious faiths, or "points of view".

A true embodied metaphysical Vision cannot be opposed to anything. What is important for Raphael is the unveiling, through living and being, of that level of Truth which one has been able to contemplate.

Writing in the light of the Unity of Tradition Raphael's works present, calling on the reader's intuition, precise points of correspondence between Eastern and Western Teachings. These points of reference are useful for those who want to approach a comparative doctrinal study and to enter the spirit of the Unity of Teaching.

For those who follow either an Eastern or a Western traditional line these correspondences help us comprehend how the *Philosophia Perennis* (Universal Tradition), which has no history and has not been formulated by human minds as such, «comprehends universal truths that do not belong to any people or any age». It is only for lack of "comprehension" or of "synthetic vision" that one particular Branch is considered the only reliable one. Such a position can but lead to opposition and fanaticism. What can degenerate the Doctrine is either a sentimental, fanatical devotion or condescending intellectualism, which is critical and sterile, dogmatic and separative.

In Raphael's words: «For those of us who aim at Realization, our task is to get to the essence of every Doctrine, because we know that just as Truth is one, so Tradition is one even if, just like Truth, Tradition may be viewed from a plurality of apparently different points of view. We must abandon all disquisitions concerning the phenomenal process of becoming, and move onto the plane of Being. In other words: we must have a Philosophy of Being as the foundation of our search and of our realization»[1].

---

[1] See, Raphael, *Tat tvam asi*, That thou art, Aurea Vidyā, New York.

Raphael interprets spiritual practice as a "Path of Fire". Here is what he writes: «...The "Path of Fire" is the pathway each disciple follows in all branches of Tradition; it is the Way of Return. Therefore, it is not the particular teaching of an individual nor a path parallel to the one and only Main Road... After all, every disciple follows his own "Path of Fire", no matter which Branch of Tradition he belongs to».

In Raphael's view, what is important is to express through living and being the truth that one has been able to contemplate. Thus, for each being, one's expression of thought and action must be coherent and in agreement with one's own specific *dharma*.

After more than thirty-five years of teaching, both oral and written, Raphael is now dedicating himself only to those people who wish to be "doers" rather than "sayers", according to St. Paul's expression.

Raphael is connected with the *maṭha* founded by *Śrı Ādi* Śaṅkara at Śṛṅgeri and Kāñcıpuram as well as with the Rāmaṇa Āśram at Tiruvannamalai.

Founder of the Āśram Vidyā Order, he now dedicates himself entirely to spiritual practice. He lives in a hermitage connected to the *āśram* and devotes himself completely to a vow of silence.

* * *

May the Raphael Consciousness, expression of Unity of Tradition, guide and illumine along this Opus all those who donate their *mens informalis* (non-formal mind) to the attainment of the highest known Realization.

GLOSSARY

Abhāva (m): Non-existence. Opposite of *bhāva*.

Advaitavāda (m): Metaphysical doctrine of Non-duality formulated by Gauḍapāda and Śaṅkara.

Adharma (m): Not in conformity with the *dharma*, that which violates the universal Order or the Law (*dharma*).

Adhyāsa (m): Superimposition, substitution. For Śaṅkara: «Appearance in a given place of something which is known from elsewhere, on the basis of imaginative projection».

Adhyātma (n): The supreme Self (*paramātman*), the principial *ātman*, or primordial Self. The intimate Self-*ātman* of all beings.

Adhyātmavidyā (f): The Knowledge of the first principles or of the universal or primordial Self. Supreme Knowledge.

Adṛṣṭa (a, n): The "not seen", the invisible. Principle non-perceived and non-perceivable by any faculty.

A-dvaita (n): Non-duality, absence of duality. (a): Without-a-second.

Advaita Vedānta: The non-dual *Vedānta*, codified by Gauḍapāda and Śaṅkara. Metaphysical *darśana* (perspectives) which transcends dualism (*dvaita*) as well as monism (*aikya*).

Advaitin (m): One who follows the *Advaitavāda*, he who has realized Non-duality.

Ahaṁ (m): personal pronoun I, notion of I as individualized reflection of consciousness, proceeding from the *ātman* (Self) through the mediation of the incarnate reflection of consciousness (*jīva*). Prototype of the *ahaṁkara* or "sense of ego".

Ahaṁkāra (m): Literally "what makes up the ego", or the "sense of the empirical ego". It constitutes consciousness in the individual state.

Ajāti (f): Non-generation.

Ajātivāda (m): The doctrine of "non-generation" presented by Gauḍapāda in his *Kārikā* (verse commentary) to the *Māṇ ḍūkya Upaniṣad.*

Ajāna (n): Ignorance of metaphysical order (avidyā).

Ākāśa (m, n): The "space", the universal ether which pervades the entire universe. It is the first of the five elements (*bhūta*), its characteristic being *śabda* (sound).

Ānanda (m): Absolute bliss, pure happiness, joy without objects. Condition that inheres to the awareness of the fullness of one's Being. One of the three inseparable and consubstantial aspects of the Self (*sat, cit, ānanda*).

Ānandamaya (m): made or constituted (*maya*) of beatitude (*ānanda*).

Ānandamayakośa (m): The sheath of beatitude. The innermost and subjective "casing". The seat of the *jīvā* in the deep sleep state. As it is determined as *kośa* (layer, sheath) it is already in the plane of limitations and therefore does not represent the ānanda of Brahman.

Annamaya (a): made or constituted (*maya*) of food (*anna*).

Annamayakośa (m): The sheath of food. The outermost sheath of the Self. Gross sheath. It corresponds to the gross physical vehicle, made up in fact of food, transformed and assimilated.

Antaḥkaraṇa (n): The internal organ, the "mind" in its full extension and various modifications (*vṛtti*) which includes: *buddhi* (intellect, intuitive perception or direct discernment), *ahaṁkāra* (sense of self), *citta* (projecting memory, deposit of subconscious tendencies and predisposition) and *manas* (empirical selective mind).

Apara (a): Inferior, lesser; non supreme, relative.

Aśabda (m): The without sound. Referred to the silent *Brahma*, *Nirguṇabrahma* (without attributes), therefore beyond word-sound.

Asat (n): Non-being; non-reality, that which is not nor exists in absolute.

Asparśa (a, n): Without contact, without relation, without support, absolute.

Asparśavāda (m): The doctrine of "without contact", of non relation, expounded by Gauḍapāda in the *Māṇḍūkyakārikā*.

Asparśayoga (m): The yoga of "without contact", the yoga of pure consciousness as the non-mediated realization of the Self.

Asparśin (m): One who has realized the *Asparśayoga*, also one who follows the *Asparśavāda*.

Āśrama (m): Hermitage, life stage. The four life stages in the traditional Hindu society are: *brahmacārya* (celibacy and study), *gṛhasthya* (social and family responsibility), *vānaprasthya* (hermit stage), *saṁnyāsa* (total renunciation). States of consciousness which determine the corresponding life stages.

Ātmabodha (m): Consciousness of the *ātman*, knowledge of the Self, title of one of Śaṅkara's treatises *(prakaraṇa)* considered as fundamental for the knowledge of the Advaita Vedānta.

Ātman (n): Self, Spirit, pure Consciousness, ontological I. *Ātman* is the absolute in us, completely outside of time-space-cause, and as such is identical to *Brahman*. Absolute in itself.

AUM (m): The sacred syllable OM (*oṁkāra*) in its constituent elements. It symbolizes the Absolute, see OM.

Avasthātraya (n): The three "states": waking-gross (*Viraṭ*), dream-subtle (*Hiraṇyagarbha*), deep sleep-causal (*Īśvara*) on which the *Vedānta* leads its investigation-discernment (*viveka*) to attain to the ultimate Reality or Fourth (*Turīya*).

Avasthātrayasākṣin (m): Witness of the three states; the Self (*ātman*), pure Consciousness without modifications.

Avidyā (f): Metaphysical ignorance, ignorance with regard to Reality, the noumenon, or the nature of Being. It is the individualized aspect of the universal ignorance, or *māyā*.

Avyakta (n): The undifferentiated, non-manifested condition of the Principle, universal One, undifferentiated condition of *prakṛti*-substance before it manifests.

Āvṛti (f): Veiling. Also *āvaraṇa*.

Bhakta (m): Devout. One who follows the path of devotion (*bhakti*). Person full of love for the Divine.

Bhakti (f): Ardent devotion, love for the Divine. Participation in the divine Being to the attainment of perfect union with It. For Śaṅkara, *bhakti* is «the constant search for one's real nature». We have *aparabhakti* (non-supreme *bhakti*) and *parabhakti* (supreme *bhakti*).

Bhaktiyoga (m): The *yoga* of devotion. The *sādhanā* rests on filling the emotional body with love so as to cause "breaking through the level", which is necessary to attain the union with the Beloved.

Bhāva (m): Birth, phenomenal existence.

Bhūta (n): The existent, constituting substance, primordial element. First elements of nature. The five sensible elements out of which all bodies are made: earth, water, fire, air, ether.

Bodha (m): Intuitive knowledge, knowledge in that consciousness.

Brahmā (m): One of the three aspects of the Hindu *Trimūrti* or the threefold form with which the qualified Being, *Brahman Saguṇa* or *Īśvara*, manifests. It is the manifesting principle of the universe that corresponds to the creator aspect, in relation with the conservator (*Viṣṇu*) and the transforming one (*Śiva*).

Brahmacārin (m): Person living the student stage of life (*āsrama*).

Brahmacarya (n): The first of the four traditional stages of life (*āsrama*), that of celibate and student (*brahmacārin*).

Brahman or *Brahma* (n): Is the absolute Reality, the Absolute in itself. "That" (*Tat*), which is totally transcendent and unconditioned, always identical to itself. One-without-a-second.

Brahman Nirguṇa or *Nirguṇabrahma* (n, m): Non-qualified Reality, free from attributes (*guṇas*), absolute. It is applied to the absolute *Brahman*, see also *Brahman*.

Brahman Saguṇa or *Saguṇabrahma* (n, m): Qualified Being, with attributes (*guṇas*). First qualification of *Brahman* (*Nirguṇa*),. See also *Īśvara*.

Brāhmaṇa (n): First of the four traditional social orders (*varṇa*), the sacerdotal one. Liturgical exegesis texts annexed to the *Veda*.

Bṛhadāraṇyaka Upaniṣad: The "*Upaniṣad* of the great *Āraṇyaka*" one of the oldest and most important Vedic *Upaniṣad*. It contains the *mahāvākya* (great aphorism) «*aham brahmāsmi*: I am *Brahman*».

Buddhi (n): Superior intellect, discerning intelligence, pure reason, intuition of the universal.

Buddhimayakośa: see *Vijñānamayakośa*

Caitanya (n): Consciousness. Spirit. Absolute pure Intelligence.

Cakra (n): "Wheel", "center". The *cakra* represent determinations of the energy-awareness, or *śakti*.

Cit (n): Pure and Absolute Consciousness (*caitanya*), pure Awareness, pure Intelligence, pure Knowledge. *Cit* is beyond any cognitive, representative process, beyond the mental and even beyond pure intellection or intellectual intuition (*buddhi*); yet it gives life to the mind itself, it provides support to its modifications and its functioning. One of the three inseparable and consubstantial aspects of the Self (*sat, cit, ānanda*).

Darśana (n): Occasion in which to contemplate a Sage. "Perspective", the term is used in relation to the *Veda* doctrine and to the six orthodox school of Hindu traditional philosophy. The six schools are: *Sāṁkhya, Yoga, Vaiśeṣika, Nyāya, Pūrva Mīmānsā* and *Uttara Mīmānsā* or *Vedānta*.

Deva (m): One who is resplendent, angelic being, Deity.

Dharma (m): Stems from the root *dhr*, which indicates supporting, preserving, "wearing", it designates in general terms a "way of being", i.e. the essential nature of a being. Therefore, conformity with the Principle in accordance with the universal law of Equilibrium-Harmony. In metaphysical terms, that through which Harmony manifests as expression of the Unity of Being. In the individual order it relates to the action which one will be able to perform in accordance with the Principle (*karmadharma*), to attain liberation. Fundamental *dharma* of each human being is to become aware of and to realize in practice one's own divine Nature, which permeates all beings.

Dṛśya (f): the visible, the object of vision or knowledge. The "spectacle" of which the *ātman* is the "spectator" or witness.

Dvaita (n, a): Duality, dualism; dualistic school; dual.

Epistéme (n, Greek anct.): Knowledge, science-consciousness.

Gauḍapāda: Master of the *Advaita Vedānta* of which he was the first codifier. Śaṅkara's spiritual Master. Author of the *Māṇḍūkyakārikā* (or *Gauḍapādīyakārikā*), verse commentary to the *Māṇḍūkya Upaniṣad*, where the *Ajātivāda* (doctrine of the non-generation, non-creation) and the *Asparśayoga* (*yoga* of no support) are exposed.

Gnosis: (n, Greek anct.): knowledge, knowledge of metaphysical import, the equivalent of *vidyā* (see also *jñāna*).

Gṛhastha (m): The second of the traditional stages of life (*āśrama*). He who lives the state of head of family; the state of who fulfills his responsibilities.

Guṇa (m): "Thread", "rope", "constituent quality", (pl.): principial attributes of *prakṛti*-substance or qualitative principles of the universal substance which are at the base of manifestation.

Guru (m): Instructor, spiritual Teacher (*ācārya*), one who removes (*ru* stands for removing) ignorance (*gu* stands for obscurity or ignorance). Instructor in the *Veda*, performs purifying ceremonies.

Haṭhayoga (m): *Yoga* of the physiological well-being. Aims at perfection and dominion of the body, for its transformation into the Temple of the Spirit.

Hiraṇyagarbha (m): Golden germ, cosmic egg (*brahmāṇḍa*). The second of the three states of Being. The totality of the subtle universal manifestation, which comprehends its individual corresponding subtle aspect (*taijasa*).

Indriya (n): Literally "power", indicates both the faculty of the senses and their corporeal organs. Together they constitute an instrument of knowledge (*jñānendriya*) and of action (*karmendriya*). The internal modification of the mind associated with the sensory organ itself.

Īśvara (m): "Divine Person", it represents what we could define as the personified God. It is the first determination of the absolute *Brahman*, and it comprehends the entire field of manifestation: gross, subtle and causal, both from the cosmic and individual points of view.

Jāgrat (n): Waking state. The other ones are: *svapna* or dream state, *suṣupti* dreamless sleep state and *Turīya*, which transcends them all.

Jīva (m): Living being (*jīvin*), individuated Soul, consciential reflection of the *ātman* on the universal plane. It produces movement and activity within itself and engenders, through *ahaṁkāra,* the subject (self-*aham*) as well as the object (world-*idam*) of experience, of knowledge.

Jīvanmukta (m): "Liberated during life", one who has extinguished the threefold Fire.

Jīvātman (m): The *ātman* reflected in the *jīva.*

Jñāna (n): Knowledge, from *jñā* (to know), identical to the Greek *gnosis*. Cathartic, liberating knowledge. Also one of the qualities of the Lord (*Bhagavad*): wisdom, intelligence.

Jñānayoga (m): The *yoga* of Knowledge. Its postulates are: intuitive discernment (*viveka)* between real (Self-*ātman)* and non-real (empirical self, non-Self), detachment (*vairāgya*) and, reintegration into the Absolute through Knowledge-awareness.

Jñāni (m): Knower, one who practices the *Jñānayoga*, realized being.

Kāma (m): Desire, coveting, greed, attachment to the sensorial world.

Kāma-manas (n): Mental condition of complete conformity with desire; relationship between desire and empirical mind; emotion that proceeds from imagination. It is the characteristic of *manomayakosa*.

Karma or *Karman* (n): Action, activity, principle of causality, effects resulting from an action; rite. It is the inertia of the mental mass of the subject which pushes it to act, think, identify and be in a specific condition. It can be considered as "cause" and as "effect" of the action, which forces the being into perennial becoming (*saṁsāra*).

Kośa (m): Shell, envelope, sheath, energetic sheath. According to *Vedānta* five sheaths envelop the Self: *ānandamayakośa, vijñānamayakośa, manomayakośa, prāṇomayakośa* and *annamayakośa*.

Kṣatriya (m): He who belongs to the regal-military order, to the order of the judges and the politicians, he who supports law and justice; one of the four traditional social orders (*varṇ a*); it corresponds to the guardians of Plato's *Politèia*. Cp. *Bhagavadgītā*.

Kuṇḍalinī (f): Literally the "rolled up". Serpentine force; nervous and psychic force placed in the lotus at the base of the spine (*mūlādhāracakra*).

Laya (m): Dissolution-transformation, destruction, absorption (see *Pralaya*).

Liṅga (n): Subtle character, reason. Phallus as symbol of energy. Its elliptic form with its two poles represents the Dyad, the bipolarity expressed in creation.

Māhāt (n): The "Great"; cosmic Intelligence; the great Mind. Principle of the cosmic manifestation according to the *Sāṁkhya darśana*. First effect of *mūlaprakṛti*.

Mahāvākya (m): Great aphorism; the Vedic great aphorisms in which the *Vedānta* Doctrine is synthesized. The main *mahāvākya* are four: *aham brahmāsmi*, I am *Brahman* (*Bṛihadāraṇyaka Up*.: I, IV, 10; of "black" *Yajur Veda*); *Tat tvam asi*, That thou art (*Chāndogya Up*.: VI, VII, 7; of *Sāma Veda*); *Prajñānaṁ Brahma*, *Brahman* is *pure* consciousness (*Aitareya Up*.: V, 3; of *Ṛg Veda*); *Ayam ātmā brahma*, This *ātman* is *Brahman* (*Māṇḍūkya Up*.: II; of *Atharva Veda*). The *mahāvākya* must be meditated upon in the light of supraconscious intuition (*buddhi*) and not be object of rational analysis of the empirical mind (*manas*).

Manas (n): Mind, internal sense, individuated empirical mind endowed of rational-analytical ability, imaginative mind.

Manomayakośa (m): The sheath constituted by the empirical mind, selective-instinctual mind that operates through attraction-repulsion. In it, is active the sense of ego (*ahaṁkāra*).

Mantra (m): Section of the *Veda*, power words or sounds, hymns used in ritual acts, sacred word, formulae or verses expressed or meditated on during concentration and meditation, vibrating thought.

Manvantara (m): Period of *Manu*, cosmic cycle that comprehends four *yuga*: *satya*, *tretā*, *dvāpara*, *kali*.

Mātrā (f): "Measure"; metric quantity; length of each foot (*pāda*), in the sense of paragraph, division, part.

Māyā (f): Metaphysical ignorance, the world of names and forms as vital phenomenon; all that is modification superimposed (*upādhi*) on the pure Consciousness of the Self; "conformed movement", *Īśvara*'s "sleep dream".

Mokṣa (m): Liberation, the attainment of eternal Beatitude as outcome of the recognition of the ultimate Truth; deliverance from ignorance (*avidyā*) from relativity-becoming and from all that constitutes *māyā* as the superimposed modification on the pure Consciousness of the *ātman*; the last of the four *puruṣārtha*.

Mumukṣutva (n, f): Intense aspiration for delivery from all bondage; longing for liberation as result of maturity of consciousness. In the *Vedānta* path, it is one of the four necessary means to penetrate the world of causes and break the chain of the superimpositions that veil Reality. Also *mumukṣutā*.

Muni (m): Ascetic person practicing silence. One who knows the value of silence (*mauna*). State of consciousness of one who has realized the non qualified Absolute.

Nāma (n): Name; complementary to *rūpa*, form. According to Vedānta, that which has a name and also a form and vice versa. The dyad *nāmarūpa* is what makes the differentiated and individuated being emerge from the substratum of unqualified Being. As Śaṅkara states, *nāma-rūpa* are mere mental modifications.

Namarūpa (n): "Name-form". The world of names and of forms that constitute becoming; constitutive elements; elements that constitute and characterize individuality.

Neti neti: "not this, not this". Aphorism of consciousness negation through which the *jñānayogin* successively discards all that is appearance as relative and transitory, and through discernment (*viveka*) and detachment (*vairāgya*) attains *Brahman*, permanent and absolute Substratum.

Nirguṇa (a): Free from *guṇa*, non-qualified, absolute, it is applied to *Brahman*.

Nirguṇabrahma (n, m): see *Brahman Nirguṇa*.

Nirvāṇa (n): Extinction, solution. Also *nivṛtti*. Supreme state in which the *jīva* has resolved into the non-dual *ātman*.

Nirvikalpa (a): Free from differentiation, immutable, absolute, transcendent. It refers to *Brahman* Consciousness, non-dual, eternal and unchanging.

Nirvikalpasamādhi (m): *Samādhi* free from differentiations. Consciousness totally free from differentiations and, therefore, from duality.

OM: The sacred syllable among all. Symbol of the Absolute, of *Brahman* and also of all the concepts the human being has of the Supreme, the Divine. This syllable is part of almost all *mantra*. The symbol itself is the symbol of Totality and of absolute Unity (non-duality) and is regarded as sacred in all of India. The syllable OM (*oṁkāra*) is seed of meditation as well as its parts A, U, M which express the gross, subtle and causal planes respectively. OM with "sound" represents the qualified Being, *Brahman Saguṇa*, while the "silent" OM represents the non qualified Being or *Brahman Nirguṇa*.

Pāda (m, n): "Foot" in the sense of paragraph, division, part. "Measure", in rhythmical poetry.

Para (a): Other, different; superior, supreme.

Paramātman (n): the Supreme Self which is identical to *Brahman*; supreme Spirit.

Paravidyā (f): Supreme Knowledge, science of the Greater Mysteries, metaphysical Knowledge.

Prājña (m): Causal body of the human *jīva*. In *prājña* multiplicity and duality are reintegrated into unity of undifferentiated consciousness, as synthesis of knowledge. It also represents the *jīva* in the deep sleep state (*suṣupti*).

Prakṛti (f): nature, universal substance, *natura naturans*, the substance by which all sensible and intelligible forms are made. For *Vedānta* it is the equivalent of *māyā*, *pradhāna* or *avyakta*.

Pralaya (m): Dissolution; return into undifferentiated state; dissolution of the manifestation, at the end of a "day" of *Brahmā* (*kalpa*).

Prāṇa (m): Vital breath, cosmic breath, vital energy.

Prāṇamayakośa (m): Sheath of the vital energy. It is constituted by the subtle energies that keep the gross body alive and active.

Praṇava (m): "That which is pronounced". The sacred syllable OM.

Prasthānatraya (n): Threefold Testimony. The threefold Science of *Vedānta* constituted by the classical *Upaniṣad*, the *Brahmasūtra* and the *Bhagavadgītā*.

Puruṣa (m): Being, man, person, Self, Spirit. For *Sāṁkhya* is the positive principle-pole correlated to *prakṛti* or negative principle-pole. With its pure presence it stimulates *prakṛti*'s activity. In union with *prakṛti* it stimulates the world. So *prakṛti* manifests the dynamism inherent to *puruṣa*'s staticity.

Rajas (n): One of the three *guṇa* (the other two are *tamas* and *sattva*) which corresponds to activity, energy, desire, fire, passion and responds to expansion, dynamic movement and development.

Rūpa (n): Grace, beauty, splendor; nature, character, peculiarity; form, quality, essence; color; forms through which life manifests. See *nāma* and *nāmarūpa*. One of the five *tanmātra* or sensible qualities: the color-form which is characteristic of the *tejas* (fire) element·

Śabda (m): The sound, verbal testimony, qualified aspect of *Brahma* in its sound OM, one of the five *tanmātra*.

Sādhanā (f): Name given to any discipline which is ardently followed with perseverance in order to progress in the spiritual life, ascesis, spiritual effort undergone for realization by the disciple.

Saguṇa (a): With attributes, qualified; it refers to *Brahman* endowed of attributes (*guṇa*) or the qualified Being, first superimposition on *Nirguṇabrahma*. Equivalent to *Īśvara*.

Saguṇabrahma (n, m): see *Brahman Saguṇa*.

Śakti (f): Energy, virtual power of *māyā*, energy of manifestation, dynamic energy induced by the presence of the positive immobile pole (*Śiva*), name of the divine mother as divine primordial energy.

Sākṣin (m): Witness, spectator that does not participate and is detached from experiential events and empirical knowledge. It refers to *ātman* as Witness of the three states.

Śama (m): Mental calm; tranquility of the mind which has stopped adhering to the outer and inner objects; cessation of mental projections, extinction of thought movement. One of the qualities, part of the third qualification, of the advaita disciple.

Samādhi (m): Its etymology means transcendent identity, which transcends the apparent formal distinction; state of union (*yoga*) with the personified Divine (*Īśvara*) and of identity (*aikya*) with the impersonal Divine (*Brahman*) attained by the *yogi*.

Saṁcita karma (n): Delayed effect or result of past actions (*karma)* which has accumulated but not reached maturation and actualization in the present state of realization, which can be easily destroyed.

Saṁnyāsa (m): Total renunciation, the last of the four traditional life stages (*āśrama*). State of consciousness in which the non-reality of the qualifications is recognized.

Saṁnyāsin (m): Renouncing ascetic. One who, having comprehended, has renounced everything.

Saṁprasāda (m): Constant and imperturbable serenity. *Pax Profunda*.

Saṁsāra (m): Perennial cycle of becoming; transmigrating within becoming as continual passage through different consciential conditions and therefore of existence; indefinite succession of birth-life-rebirth to which liberation (*mokṣa)* puts an end. It corresponds to the uninterrupted chain of cause-effect, for which *karma* ties the individual to becoming.

Saṁskāra (m): 1. Preparatory purification rites, for consecration, clothing, etc., preparatory rites in general.

2. Causal "seeds" of action engendered by the tendencies that are present in the mental substance (*citta*) and deriving from experiences, actions, thoughts produced in the present existence as well as in the innumerable prior ones.

Śaṅkara: 1. Codifier of the *Advaita Vedānta*, metaphysical *darśana* which transcends the religious dualism and ontological monism itself. He lived between 788 and 820 A.D. Compiled important commentaries (*bhāṣya*) to numerous *Upaniṣad*, to the *Brahmasūtra, Bhagavadgītā*, and other works in which he summarizes the teaching and the practice through which to attain *Advaita* realization. He was a disciple of Govindapāda who in turn was a disciple of Gauḍapāda. He established himself as a strenuous defender of the *Sanātanadharma*, the Doctrine of the pure Vedic Tradition, and instituted ten monastic orders to prevent degeneration of spiritual practice. With the codifying of *Advaita* he provided a solid ontological and metaphysical base for all the cults of the time. He founded four monasteries-*maṭha* at the four cardinal points of India, focal points of the very powerful influence still perceived today. 2. (m): "He who donates every sort of good", name of *Śiva* that means auspicious, propitious, benevolent, giver of joy and prosperity. *Śiva* is *Śaṅkara*, he who with his Grace causes *saṁ*, or *ānanda* at the highest level.

Śānta (a): Totally pacified, perfectly quiet.

Śāntānām : Mental calm. See *śama* and *śānta*.

Śāstra (n): Code, teaching, sacred text. It indicates all sacred Scriptures in general.

Sat (n): Being, pure Being. Absolute and pure existence, contrary to *asat*: that which has no existence. *Sat, cit, ānanda* are the three consubstantial aspects of Being.

Sat-cit-ānanda: Absolute Existence (*sat*), Consciousness (*cit*) and Bliss (*ānanda*). The three consubstantial aspects of *Brahman* and therefore of *ātman*.

Sattva (n): Being, existence in itself, essence, wisdom, "intellectual light", one of the three *guṇa* (the other two are *rajas* and *tamas*) which corresponds to equilibrium, harmony, light, purity. In the hierarchical order of manifestation it corresponds to the causal plane, *rajas* to the subtle and *tamas* to the gross one.

Savikalpa (a): With differentiation, that which contains in itself differentiation, differentiated, formal.

Savikalpa samādhi (m): Transcendental contemplation in which the distinction of subject and object is still latent. It leads to the realization of *Brahman Saguṇa*.

Śiva (m): Beneficial, propitious, one of the three aspects of the *Trimūrti*. The Divine when considered in its transforming and resolving aspect (*mūrti*), but when in union with its *śakti* (*Pārvatī*) it takes the function of creator; as such it is symbolized by the *liṅga*. Śaivism separates the aspect of creating from those of conserving and dissolving, so that the aspects that *Śiva* takes and those of the corresponding *śakti* are differentiated, but *Śiva* at the same time is considered as the sole and absolute Principle. For *Vedānta* it is the always and everywhere present One-without-a-second, i.e. *Brahman*.

Smṛti (f): Remembered, indirect or "mediated" Tradition.

Sparśa (m): Contact, relation.

Śūdra (m): One of the four traditional social orders (*varṇa*), it is equivalent of workman. He who lays the foundations of human well-being with service activities.

Śruti (f): Audition, the Tradition of the "Heard", sacred Knowledge which was "immediately" revealed (*Veda*), what was heard by the ancient Seers (*Ṛṣi*) as divine Sounds. One of the names given the *Veda*.

Suṣupti (f): State of deep sleep. Sleep without dream, corresponds to the causal body-plane.

Sūtra (n): Thread, rope; aphorism, verse. Text that codifies the fundamental principles of the various philosophical *darśana*. Metaphorically, *ātman* that connects all existential planes.

Sūtrātma (n): Thread of the Self; word that equates to *Hiraṇya-garbha*, subtle universal aspect which comprises the different individualities. Consciential "continuity" of the Self.

Svapna (n): Dream, dream state.

Taijasa (m): "Luminous", from *tejas* (fire); the second quarter, *pāda* (foot) of *ātman*. It constitutes the subtle plane of formal manifest existence and therefore the threefold subtle body (*sūkṣmaśarīra*). It corresponds to *Hiraṇyagarbha* in the universal order.

Tanmātra (m): Literally "the measure of this", extension or boundary of something. It indicates the substantial quality of an object, but more specifically of the "elements" that are forming it; also what makes the experience possible through the specific and corresponding sensory organs of knowledge (*jñānendriya*).

Tamas (n): One of the three *guṇa* (the other two are *rajas* and *sattva*), which corresponds to obscurity, inertia, passiveness, to inert staticity, etc. It faces "down", it corresponds to ignorance (*avidyā*), representing the maximum condensation of the potentiality of the being. In the hierarchical order of manifestation it corresponds to the gross plane, *rajas* to the subtle and *sattva* to the causal one.

Tapas (n): Heat, ascetic heat, austerity; ardent aspiration, one of the five *niyama* of *Patañjali*'s *Rājayoga*.

Tat (pr): "That". In the *Upaniṣad* it indicates the unqualified Absolute, *Brahman* devoid of attributes or *Nirguṇabrahman*.

Tattva (n): "Quiddity", truth, principle; category, elemental principle. The twenty-five principles, categories in the *Sāṁkhya darśana*, and the twenty-six in the *Yoga darśana*.

Turīya (a, n): The Fourth, "Fourth state" (*Caturtha*) which is real absolute and constitutes the necessary non-dual substratum of all relative states and their contents. *Turīya* is *Nirguṇabrahma* and represents the Absolute, Infinite, metaphysical Zero. It can be described only by negations: Non-born, Non-caused, Non-limited, Non-conditioned, Non-determined. It is One-without-a-second (*advaita*) that comprehends and transcends all duality and even the Principle ontological unity itself (*Īśvara)*.

Upādhi (m): Superimposition, what is superimposed on the Self constituting thereby a "vehicle" and a conditioning at the same time.

Upaniṣad (n): "Sessions or esoteric teaching". Act of "sitting next to someone" in reverential attitude, referring to the disciple at the feet of the Master receiving esoteric knowledge, secret wisdom. For Śaṅkara their purpose is to destroy ignorance-*avidyā*, by providing means apt to attain supreme Knowledge.

Vairāgya (n): Detachment from every form of fruit of action, from all conditions and all objects of attachment; renunciation founded on personal reflection and on the teaching from the *guru*.

Vaiśvānara (m): Totality of existence at the gross state of manifestation. Gross totality (*Virāṭ*). It corresponds on the universal plane to the individual gross-physical body (*viśva)*. First state of Being described in the *Māṇḍūkya Upaniṣad*: Self in the waking state.

Vaiśya (m): The third of the traditional social orders (*varṇa*), that of the producers of wealth.

Vaitathya: Apparent, illusory.

Vānaprasthya (n): The third of the traditional stages of life (*āśrama*). State of he who, having done its duty as head of family, retires into a life of renunciation and meditation. It is a state of consciousness in which the withdrawal from the world is motivated by the *jīva*'s maturity and not by the escape from one's own duties.

Varṇa (m): Color, social order. The four traditional social orders: *brāhmana* (sacerdotes), *kśatriya* (lawmakers or warriors), *vaiśya* (producers of wealth) and *śūdra* (workmen). Also one of the three types of sound (see *śabda*).

Vāsanā (f): Subconscious mental impression induced by experience, action and thought, or arising out of indefinite epochs of the past through accumulated *karma*. "Furrows" in the mental substance (*citta*), they constitute the true "seeds" (*saṁskāra*) of thought, and also of rebirth.

Veda (m): Literally "what has been seen, realized by sages (*Ṛṣi*)"; supreme Knowledge, sacred Science. The four great collections: *Ṛg Veda, Sāma Veda, Yajur Veda* and *Atharva Veda*, contain the exposition of that sacred and traditional Science in its highest expressions and form the *Śruti*.

Vedānta (m): "The accomplishment of the *Veda*". One of the six *darśana*, also called *Uttara Mīmāṁsā*. It encompasses three currents:

1. *Advaita Vedānta* (non-dualism) codified by Śaṅkarācārya;
2. *Viśiṣṭādvaita*, also *Bhedābheda* (qualified monism) codified by Rāmānuja;
3. *Dvaitavedānta* (dualism) codified by Madhva.

Vidyā (f): Knowledge of Reality; consciousness meditation that leads to realization, classified as lower (*apara*) and higher (*para*). The *aparavidyā* is in relation with the first three ends of the human being: *dharma* or rectitude, *artha* or well being, *kāma* or legitimate desire. The *paravidyā*, expounded in the *Upaniṣad*, regards the ultimate end of the human being: *mokṣa* or liberation.

Vijñāna (n): Pure intellect, synonym of *buddhi*, as "synthetic-integrating knowledge" in relation with *manas*. Also Knowledge in the sense of awareness-consciousness.

Vijñānamayakośa (m): Sheath made of intellect, envelope of superior intellect, or *buddhi*. Its nature is represented by intellective reason, intuitive discernment. When developed it balances *manomayakośa*, when made "*sattvic*" it is able to contemplate universal archetypes.

Vikṣepaśakti (f): The projective power of *avidyā-māyā* through which, in place of the Real, it projects the image of the universe of names and forms. It is related to *āvṛtiśakti* (veiling power).

Virāṭ or *Virāj* (m): The totality of the gross manifestation (*vaiśvānara*).

Viśva (n): Represents totality of gross manifestation; consciousness waking state in the individual order.

Viveka (m): Intuitive discernment, discrimination between real and non-real, noumenon and phenomenon, which leads to detachment (*vairāgya*) from the non-real and to becoming conscious of Reality.

Vivekacūḍāmaṇi: "The Great Jewel of Discernment", title of a work by Śrī Śaṅkarācārya which is a fundamental text for the realization of the *Advaita Vedānta*. In it a dialogue takes place between a Master and a neophyte where all the principal aspects of the doctrine of Non-duality are thoroughly researched in a highly philosophical and poetical way, in both cognitive and operative aspects.

Yoga: 1. One of the six *darśana*, it represents the "doctrine of Union", it is not only a philosophy but proposes operative means to attain "Union".

2. (m): Union, reintegration, complete fusion. Generally the reintegration of the individual into the universal, of the relative (*jīva*) into the absolute (*ātman*).

Yogi or *Yogin* (m): One who practices *yoga*, who is advanced in *yoga*, who has attained Union, i.e. is reintegrated in the *ātman*.

PUBLICATIONS

Books by Raphael
published in English

At the Source of Life
Aurea Vidyā, New York

Beyond the illusion of the ego
Aurea Vidyā, New York

Essence and Purpose of Yoga
The Initiatory Pathways to the Transcendent
Element Books, Shaftesbury, U.K.

Initiation into the Philosophy of Plato
Aurea Vidyā, New York

Orphism and the Initiatory Tradition
Aurea Vidyā, New York

Pathway of Fire, Initiation to the Kabbalah
S. Weiser, York Beach, Maine, U.S.A.

The Pathway of Non-duality, Advaitavāda
Motilal Banarsidass, New Delhi

Tat tvam asi, That thou art,
The Path of Fire According to the Asparśavāda
Aurea Vidyā, New York

The Threefold Pathway of Fire
Aurea Vidyā, New York

Traditional Classics
in English

Śaṅkara, ***Ātmabodha****, Self-knowledge. Aurea Vidyā , New York

Śaṅkara, ***Drigdriśyaviveka****, Discernment between *ātman* and non-*ātman*. Aurea Vidyā, New York

Gauḍapāda, ***Māṇḍūkyakārikā****, The Māṇḍūkya Upaniṣad with the verses-*kārikā* of Gauḍapāda and Commentary by Raphael. Aurea Vidyā, New York

Parmenides, ***On the Order of Nature***, Περί φύσεως**, For a Philosophical Ascesis. Aurea Vidyā, New York

Śaṅkara, ***Vivekacūḍāmaṇi****, The Crest-jewel of Discernment. Aurea Vidyā, New York

Forthcoming Publications
in English

Śaṅkara, ***Aparokṣānubhūti*** *, Self-realization

Raphael, ***Science of Love***

The Bhagavadgītā *

Bādarāyaṇa, ***Brahmasūtra*** *, **

Five Upaniṣad * Īśa, Kaivalya, Sarvasāra, Amṛtabindu, Atharvaśira

Raphael, ***Fire of Awakening***

Patañjali, ***The Regal Way to Realization,*** Yogadarśana *

*Translation from the Sanskrit, and commentary, by Raphael

** Edited by Raphael

Aurea Vidyā is the Publishing House of the Parmenides Traditional Philosophy Foundation, a Not-for-Profit Organization whose purpose is to make Perennial Philosophy accessible.

The Foundation goes about its purpose in a number of ways: by publishing and distributing Traditional Philosophy texts with Aurea Vidyā, by offering individual and group encounters and by providing a Reading Room and daily Meditations at its Center.

* * *

Those readers who have an interest in Traditional Philosophy are welcome to contact the Foundation at the address shown on the colophon page.

CPSIA information can be obtained at www.ICGtesting.com
Printed in the USA
BVOW07s2250240713

326924BV00001B/26/P